General editor: Graham Handley

Brodie's Notes on Henry Fielding's

Tom Jones

Graham Handley MA PhD
Formerly principal lecturer in English, College of All Saints, Tottenham

MACMILLAN

© The Macmillan Press Ltd 1987

All rights reserved. No reproduction, copy or transmission of
this publication may be made without written permission.

No paragraph of this publication may be reproduced, copied or
transmitted save with written permission or in accordance with
the provisions of the Copyright, Designs and Patents Act 1988,
or under the terms of any licence permitting limited copying
issued by the Copyright Licensing Agency, 90 Tottenham Court
Road, London W1P 9HE.

Any person who does any unauthorised act in relation to this
publication may be liable to criminal prosecution and civil
claims for damages.

First published 1987 by Pan Books Ltd

Reprinted 1992 by
THE MACMILLAN PRESS LTD
Houndmills, Basingstoke, Hampshire RG21 2XS
and London
Companies and representatives
throughout the world

ISBN 0-333-58090-7

Printed in Great Britain by
Clays Ltd, St Ives plc, Bungay, Suffolk

Contents

References in these notes are to the Penguin Classics edition of *Tom Jones* but as each chapter is analysed separately, the Notes may be used with any edition of the book.

Preface by the general editor

The intention throughout this study aid is to stimulate and guide, to encourage your involvement in the book, and to develop informed responses and a sure understanding of the main details.

Brodie's Notes provide a clear outline of the play or novel's plot, followed by act, scene, or chapter summaries and/or commentaries. These are designed to emphasize the most important literary and factual details. Poems, stories or non-fiction texts combine brief summary with critical commentary on individual aspects or common features of the genre being examined. Textual notes define what is difficult or obscure and emphasize literary qualities. Revision questions are set at appropriate points to test your ability to appreciate the prescribed book and to write accurately and relevantly about it.

In addition, each of these Notes includes a critical appreciation of the author's art. This covers such major elements as characterization, style, structure, setting and themes. Poems are examined technically – rhyme, rhythm, for instance. In fact, any important aspect of the prescribed work will be evaluated. The aim is to send you back to the text you are studying.

Each study aid concludes with a series of general questions which require a detailed knowledge of the book: some of these questions may invite comparison with other books, some will be suitable for coursework exercises, and some could be adapted to work you are doing on another book or books. Each study aid has been adapted to meet the needs of the current examination requirements. They provide a basic, individual and imaginative response to the work being studied, and it is hoped that they will stimulate you to acquire disciplined reading habits and critical fluency.

Graham Handley 1991

The author and his work

Henry Fielding was the son of an army lieutenant (later to be promoted) and was born at Sharpham Park, the home of his grandfather on his mother's side, on 22 April 1707. This home of the future novelist was near Glastonbury in Somerset but when he was six the family moved to East Stour, close to Shaftesbury in Dorset, and here his younger sister Sarah, also to become a celebrated writer, was born.

Henry's mother died when he was eleven, and after his father married again the boy was sent to Eton, having previously had a private tutor. It is thought that the character of Parson Adams in *Joseph Andrews* was based on this tutor, a clergyman by the name of Oliver. At Eton Fielding became friendly with George (later Lord) Lyttleton and with Pitt the elder, later first Earl of Chatham, the great Whig statesman prominent in the 1760s and 70s. He studied hard at Eton, acquiring that detailed familiarity with the classics that is evident from his work. By the age of eighteen he had his first serious love affair, attempting to elope with the girl when he was nineteen. He failed, the girl was taken away to Devon; Fielding, perhaps by way of compensation, settled in London. He was intent upon becoming a successful dramatist, and in 1728 his first play, *Love in Several Masques*, was successfully produced at Drury Lane.

After this Fielding left England and spent two years studying at Leiden University in Holland but when he returned to London he still sought out the theatre as his livelihood, precarious though that turned out to be. Between 1729 and 1737 Fielding wrote about twenty-five pieces; all in a comic vein, some farcical, some satirical, always with an element of the burlesque. Two of his plays were adapted from the work of the French writer Molière, but he was also influenced by the great Restoration dramatist William Congreve. He satirized the pantomime and opera, the law in the person of Justice Squeezum in *Rape Upon Rape*, but his most successful play was undoubtedly *The Tragedy of Tragedies; or The Life and Death of Tom Thumb the Great*, an extravagant flight in the burlesque manner of Buckingham's *The Rehearsal*. At about this time his friendship with the great painter and engraver William Hogarth began. Fielding characteristically showed his admiration for the outstanding Spanish writer Cervantes through his satire of *Don Quixote*.

In 1734 Fielding married Charlotte Cradock, with whom he was to spend ten happy years before her death in 1744. There is no doubt that she was the model for two of his heroines, Sophia Western in *Tom Jones* and Amelia in the novel of that name. Helped by his friends – particularly Lyttleton – he survived periods of poverty, and there is little doubt that his friendship with Ralph Allen ('The Man of Bath') led to his conceiving the character of Mr Allworthy in *Tom Jones*. He became manager of the New Theatre in London's Haymarket, and for the opening he wrote the successful satire *Pasquin* which exposed religious and political chicanery and also mocked the theatre and the social manners of the day. But an even fiercer satire caused a government reaction, which led to the Licensing Act of 1737. This effectively finished Fielding's career as a dramatist, and he returned to his legal studies.

He entered the Middle Temple, and was called to the Bar in 1740. He continued to write, contributing satirical articles to *The Champion*, an anti-Jacobite journal (see the section on the historical background to *Tom Jones*) and Fielding's squibs appeared under his pseudonym of Captain Hercules Vinegar. He edited other journals of the same kind over the next few years; among his concerns were the conditions of the prisons and the nature of life within them; the administration of the poor laws; gambling and drinking.

Fielding's new career was already at hand. In 1741 Samuel Richardson's novel *Pamela* appeared. It was immediately successful, but Fielding's reaction to its stern sexual morality (to be seduced is a sin, to hold out for marriage is a virtue) was to publish *An Apology for the Life of Mrs Shamela Andrews* in the same year, though under the pseudonym of Conny Keyber. He followed this with a more direct attack; the hero of his next book was the virtuous Pamela's supposed brother, equally virtuous but subjected to various assaults on his virtue. It is a richly comic performance; Fielding had found his *métier*: the humour, the earthiness, the social foreground and the range of characterization are all impressive. This was followed in 1743 by *The Life and Death of Jonathan Wild the Great*. This fierce satire castigated political hypocrisy and scheming, fake virtue and the many sins of humanity. Admiration for criminals comes under the whip. Fielding knew the life of which he was writing, and there is a running realism that is both graphic and savage.

Fielding's health had never been good, and about this time he began to suffer acutely from gout. The terrible blow of his wife's death apparently turned him away from literature for a time, though he wrote a preface for his sister's novel *David Simple*. In 1746, however, Fielding began *Tom Jones*, and in the following year he married his dead wife's maid Mary Daniel. They had a son in 1748 and in the same year Fielding was appointed a Justice of the Peace for

Westminster, and in 1749 for Middlesex. Now he was able to operate against the corruptions of the law from the inside, being particularly severe on judges who were given to embezzling the fines they imposed.

Tom Jones was published in 1749, to great public acclaim but little literary praise, Richardson and Dr Johnson being among those who objected to its coarseness and realism. The omniscient author imparted his ideas, his literary, moral and philosophical outlook, and in so doing he sired the direct line of the English novel. The richness of the characterization, the attack on humbug and hypocrisy, the humour, the generous feelings and the graphic action, all combine to make *Tom Jones* a great novel. The social range alone is impressive, for he covers, to use Walter Besant's phrase, all sorts and conditions of men. Good triumphs over evil, but there is no pure good in the novel. Tom has his taints, but he is all the more human for their possession.

Meanwhile Fielding, with his brother Sir John, who was almost blind, continued his attack on the corruptions of society from Bow Street. He did his utmost to elevate the law by insisting on standards of honesty and integrity. Everywhere his humanity is evident. He even, well ahead of his time, wrote a pamphlet proposing the abolition of public executions. In 1751 his final novel *Amelia* was published and, like *Tom Jones*, was an immediate success, despite the now predictable reaction of the literary establishment. Fielding, having suffered a severe deterioration in his health, remained active. Another proposal seeking to ameliorate the condition of the poor reflects the deep-rooted nature of his humanism. In addition to gout Fielding was now suffering from dropsy and asthma. He was too ill to travel to Bath to try the waters, and was frequently seen on crutches. In 1754 he and his wife sailed for Lisbon in the hope that the climate would effect an improvement. He has left an account of this journey in *The Journal of a Voyage to Lisbon*, a book which is informed with liveliness of observation despite its author's low physical state; it also reflects his courage.

Fielding died in Lisbon on 8 October 1754 and was buried in the English cemetery there. He had given himself to life, to literature and to the law; endured poverty, personal loss and criticism. But he maintained a constant humanity of outlook, a broadly based charity, tolerance and compassion. Coming from a somewhat privileged background he showed himself to be in the van of concern for those who were less well off than himself. He came to a close knowledge of the criminal classes on whom he so often sat in judgment. Thackeray has written of him as a man who 'retains some of the most precious and splendid human qualities and endowments. He has an admirable natural love of truth, the keenest instinctive antipathy to hypocrisy, the happiest satirical gift of laughing it to scorn.' (*Lectures on the English Humourists of the Eighteenth Century*)

Margaret Drabble has recently described Fielding as 'an innovating master of the highest originality', citing Sir Walter Scott as crediting him with 'high notions of the dignity of an art which he may be considered as having founded'. His acknowledged models were Swift and Cervantes, but Richardson was the convenient contemporary who provided him with the impulse that was to develop so fruitfully. His own description of his works as 'comic epics in prose' is too limited in its modest accuracy, since he is philosopher, moralist, psychologist, social historian and realist within the self-imposed confines of his art. Those confines could not hold his love of life and his love for his fellow men, nor the wisdom that makes for great writing. To read Fielding is to find yourself in the presence of genius but it is the genius of tolerance, humility, humour, compassion and the kindly irony that comes from experience and an inherent capacity to measure it.

The literary background and the novel

It is often asserted that the novel begins with Samuel Richardson, who published *Pamela, or Virtue Rewarded* in 1740–1. It is rather slighting to such major writers as Daniel Defoe (1660–1731) and Jonathan Swift (1667–1745), the first remembered for *Robinson Crusoe* and *Moll Flanders*, the second for *Gulliver's Travels*. Richardson certainly sparked off Fielding, so in that sense he is important. He was a printer who impregnated his writings with morality, so that Pamela manages to survive temptation and attempts at seduction, but in a calculating way. The two volumes in which she resists and finally settles somewhat archly for the wedding-ring are full of narrative tension. The story is told in the form of letters and Pamela's own account. It shows her vulgarity, her self-righteousness, her purity [in inverted commas] and her frankly materialistic motives, which make her less than a heroine. Fielding leapt at the opportunity to pillory this vein of narrative. His *Joseph Andrews* not only takes Pamela's name but also her attitude. Joseph is her brother, and he resists all attempts on his virtue. Here, before *Tom Jones*, is Fielding in mock-heroic vein. The result is ridiculous, but it is ridicule that is fun. Richardson took himself seriously; Fielding never paid him that compliment.

The other great novelists of the period are Smollett (1721–71) and Sterne (1713–68). The first was the traveller-novelist who published *Roderick Random* in 1748. He translated *Don Quixote* and later published a *History of England* which sold well despite its controversial tone. *The Expedition of Humphry Clinker* was published in 1771, a few months before his death. His novels are picaresque, full of earthy scenes, and display his passion for justice; like Fielding he revels in the exploits of his heroes. Sterne is the most idiosyncratic of all the English novelists. His two great works are *Tristram Shandy* and *A Sentimental Journey*, and in *The Oxford Companion to English Literature* we are told that 'Throughout his work he parodies, with a virtuosity that has proved inimitable, the developing conventions of the still-new "novel", and its problems in presenting reality, space and time. His sharp wit, often sly and often salacious, is balanced by the affection and tolerance he displays towards the absurdities of life.' (p.937).

These are Fielding's contemporaries, and with him they establish the pattern of the English novel. But Fielding's literary inheritance in the eighteenth century is a wide one, and we must remember that he is not only a journalist but a playwright too. [Mention is made elsewhere in this commentary of his devotion to the classics.] Fielding also refers to Shakespeare, and it was in the eighteenth century that Shakespeare enjoyed great popularity. Fielding's friend, the outstanding actor/producer David Garrick, produced acting versions of Shakespeare in which that greatest of dramatists was brought into line with the classical rule of unity of time, place and action. In the reigns of Anne (1702–14) and George I (1714–27) the poets and literary men ranked highly in society. Two famous journals, The *Tatler* and The *Spectator*, raised the standard of the essay and also the standard of the public's literary appreciation. Often, as in the cases of Defoe, Swift and Addison, literary men entered politics. It was the great age of the heroic couplet and the attendant satire of political figures. The court turned its back on the patronage of men of letters, but the opposition provided plenty of support and encouragement. The major poet was Alexander Pope, who had inherited the mantle of John Dryden. It was an age of wit and of rational and balanced expression as distinct from emotional outpouring. Another indication of the increasing power of print is seen in the growth of the number of newspapers. Authors, apart from Grub Street hacks, often made large amounts of money from their books. Pope began his translation of Homer, and found that £4000, an immense sum, had been subscribed before the work was published. This set him up for life. Fielding received £600 for *Tom Jones* and almost twice the sum for *Amelia*. Circulating libraries also furthered the sale of books.

The greatest figure of the eighteenth century is undoubtedly Dr Johnson. He established magazines like the *Idler* and the *Rambler*, wrote superb prose, had his conversation recorded by one of the greatest of biographers, James Boswell, contributed as essayist, poet, biographer of poets and, of course, produced the first great English dictionary. It has been rightly called 'a mirror of the author's robust prejudices and devastating wit', but it paved the way for subsequent lexicographers.

The political, social and religious background

With the Hanoverian succession established after the death of Queen Anne according to the Act of Settlement, the system of Cabinet Government was engineered by the great Whig Prime Minister Robert Walpole, who ruled the country effectively in the years 1721–42. But initially, with the accession of George I in 1714, there was some attempt to proclaim the Roman Catholic James III, son of James II, as King. The Jacobites, as his supporters were called, embarrassed the government during the early years of the Hanoverian reign. The Jacobites were well able to take advantage of the new King, who spoke no English, but with the putting down of the rebellion of 1715 they seemed to have lost the opportunity of taking the kingdom.

As direct background to *Tom Jones*, however, there is the resurgence of Jacobitism, which centres on the attractive personality of Charles Edward Stuart, the grandson of James II, and known as the Young Pretender. He laid his plans in France, landed in Scotland in July 1745, and roused many clansmen to his support. In September he defeated the forces under Sir John Cope at Prestonpans, and unwisely decided to invade England instead of consolidating his position in Scotland. Charles took Carlisle, exacted money from Preston and Manchester, and eventually reached Derby. But by now his own army was shrinking, few recruits were joining him, and the Duke of Cumberland was dogging his footsteps. He returned to Scotland and besieged Stirling Castle early in the New Year. Cumberland intercepted a sloop, and English cruisers stopped reinforcements arriving from France. Cumberland defeated the Highlanders at Culloden in April 1746, then proceeded to 'mop up' in Scotland with a savagery that earned him the nickname of 'The Butcher'. The fears and apprehensions – and some support for the Jacobites – are well captured as background to the central narrative of *Tom Jones*, with someone as innocent as Partridge a Jacobite supporter. A whole host of rumours and speculations attested to the atmosphere in the country. As Arnold Kettle has observed, '*Tom Jones* is a panoramic commentary on England in 1745' (*An Introduction to the English Novel*, 1951), and Fielding, by tracing the journeys of Tom, manages to convey a picture of the social life of the times. There is the constant threat of robbery and violence; there is the swindling and opportunist attitude towards money, the diversions and drums of high society.

Poor social conditions and the abuse of alcohol are both noted. There is every indication of the bad state of the roads, and the turnpike levies were heavy. The Methodist movement under the stimulus of Charles Wesley and his more famous brother John together with the influence of George Whitefield (who is referred to in *Tom Jones*), took hold of whole sections of the populace. John travelled the length and breadth of the country to preach the word, and was subjected to hostility and abuse from mobs organized by clergymen who were against his doctrines. In fact in 1741 and 1744, very close to the fictional time of *Tom Jones*, Wesley had become so celebrated that he was invited to preach by the University of Oxford. He brought about the regeneration of a living faith.

The Methodists appealed to countrymen who had never been inside a church. This occurred almost on the eve of the industrial revolution, when new communities were being born in the sordid conditions of the new factories. The Church of England was largely apathetic, having little or no contact with the poor, whereas the Methodists sought them out and gave them the hope and community of the Christian message.

The plot

Tom Jones is a comic-epic in eighteen books. Below there is a summary of the subject matter of each book, brief and to the point. This is to avoid summarizing each chapter since it is felt that a positive appreciation of the art of *Tom Jones* will be best provided by a commentary on the chapters in order to bring out points of interest in terms of character, situation, humour, background etc.

Book 1

This consists of thirteen chapters. [In the first chapter of each book the author addresses the reader on a topic of his choice.] Here he gives us some description of Squire Allworthy and his sister Bridget. The Squire, a wealthy widower, has returned from an absence in London, to find that a child has been placed in his bed. He tells Bridget that he has a present for her. She responds to the child but meanwhile a search is made for the mother. Miss Bridget's servant Deborah Wilkins decides that the likely culprit is one Jenny Jones. Summoned to Allworthy's presence, Jenny admits her guilt but refuses to name the father of the child. She is sent away.

The action now centres on Bridget Allworthy. Dr Blifil, Allworthy's friend, encourages his brother Captain Blifil to ingratiate himself with Miss Bridget. The Captain proposes to her and is accepted. The ingrate Captain then seeks to shake off the brother who has done so much to further his suit with Bridget. Dr Blifil, deeply hurt by his brother's ingratitude, goes to London, where he dies of a broken heart.

Book 2

This is somewhat shorter, comprising nine chapters. It traces the main events in the two years after the Blifil marriage. A son was born eight months after that marriage. Captain Blifil is jealous of Allworthy's attentions to the foundling Tom Jones, as he is now called. There is now retrospect on Jenny Jones, her staying with the schoolmaster Partridge, her scholarly attainments, and the jealousy of Partridge's wife. There is a fearful domestic quarrel – Mrs Wilkins learns of it and believes that Partridge is the father of Tom by Jenny. She tells Captain Blifil of this, Blifil tells Allworthy, and the latter summons

Partridge to him and condemns him. Partridge loses his school and his wife dies. Allworthy continues to show affection towards Tom; Captain Blifil waxes jealous and also begins to hate his wife. He is scheming to get Allworthy's money but before he can do so 'he himself – died of an apoplexy.'

Book 3

The ten chapters of this Book cover the period from Tom's fourteenth year to his nineteenth. He is contrasted in his naturalness and naughtiness with the falsely virtuous Master Blifil. Tom protects the gamekeeper and is flogged by Thwackum; Allworthy, convinced he has been wronged, gives Tom a little horse. Next Thwackum and Square are described (they both favour Blifil against Tom) and Blifil's character is revealed. Both Thwackum and Square cast eyes on Mrs Blifil the widow. She knows this; as Tom grows up, she favours him and not her son. Allworthy notices, and seeks to make up for this to young Blifil. Tom sells his horse in order to get money for the gamekeeper and his family. Allworthy, seeing the state they are in, promises to provide for them, but Blifil distorts a minor crime of Black George's and gets him discredited with Allworthy. Meanwhile, Tom becomes friendly with the neighbouring squire Mr Western and with his daughter Sophia.

Book 4

Fourteen chapters, with initially some emphasis on the description of Sophia Western. She is eighteen. Tom has presented her with a bird. On one occasion Blifil releases the bird. Tom climbs a tree to rescue it, but falls into a canal. Thwackum and Square debate the rights and wrongs of the incident. Western shows his roughness and his affection for Tom. Sophia is in love with Tom but doesn't know it. Tom meanwhile fancies himself in love with Molly Seagrim, Black George's daughter, who becomes pregnant. She unwisely goes to church, brings down the wrath of her neighbours upon herself, and gets involved in a churchyard battle. She is rescued by Tom and returned to her family. Parson Supple tells Western that Tom is the father of Molly Seagrim's child (and this in front of Sophia). When Tom arrives home he finds Molly being taken to a House of Correction. He tells Allworthy that he is responsible for her condition, and she is discharged. Sophia's maid Mrs Honour talks to her of Tom. Next day Sophia is thrown from her horse, but caught by Tom, who breaks his arm, which is then set by a boringly talkative surgeon. Mrs

Honour again talks to Sophia, convincing her that Jones is in love with her (Sophia).

Book 5

The events of the next twelve chapters occupy 'somewhat longer than half a year'. Sophia and Western visit Tom, and the latter notices Sophia's feelings towards him. He considers the position, and thinks of Molly. Mrs Honour acquaints him with the fact that Sophia wants to help Molly, and Jones is once more won to Sophia. He decides to give Molly money, visits her home, and finds Square in her room. He discovers that he is not after all the father of Molly's child. He cannot tell Sophia easily of his love for her – they are both emotionally overcome – but this scene gives way to the illness of Allworthy. He tells each member of his family – and Square and Thwackum – what he is leaving them. Meanwhile Mrs Blifil dies at Salisbury, Blifil tells the sick Allworthy the news, much to Tom Jones' anger. But Allworthy is soon out of crisis, and Tom celebrates. As a result of this, he quarrels with Blifil. Tom wanders off, meets Molly while he is thinking of Sophia, and retires with her (Molly) 'into the thickest part of the grove'. Thwackum and Blifil find them, a fight ensues (Molly has sneaked off), and Western appears. Blifil has been knocked senseless; Sophia faints, recovers, and gives Tom a look of tenderness for his injuries. But Squire Western mocks Tom over the 'wench' he has had, and in doing so upsets his daughter.

Book 6

The fourteen chapters of this book cover three weeks. The first opens with a discussion of love, then reveals Miss Western's opinion that Sophia is in love with Blifil. She tells Western this, and he proposes the match to Allworthy. The latter, though cautious, communicates the proposal to Blifil. A meeting with Sophia is arranged for that afternoon, but before then she tells her aunt that she cannot tolerate Blifil but is in love with Tom. Miss Western tells her brother of the love between Tom and Sophia. The squire is infuriated, tries to assault Tom, but is restrained by Parson Supple. Then Western descends upon Allworthy to tell him the news. Blifil tells Allworthy of Tom's misdemeanours with considerable distortion, and Allworthy turns Tom away, giving him (though Tom does not know this) five hundred pounds in a pocket-book. Tom writes his farewell to Sophia, drops the pocket book with the money, which is picked up by Black George, although he affects to search for it with Tom. Sophia confides again in Honour, who tells her that Jones has been turned away 'stark naked'. Sophia sends Tom money via Black George. Sophia is confined to her apartment by the squire, but her aunt arranges her release.

Book 7

Fifteen chapters, the first containing a comparison between the world and the stage. Book 7 covers three days in narrative time. Tom leaves, having determined to go to sea, while Sophia argues with her aunt against the marriage to Blifil. Blifil's next visit shows Sophia adamant and Blifil pretending to love her (he hates her, really, because of her preference for Jones). Allworthy is duped into thinking that the match ought to go ahead. Honour reveals to Sophia that a licence has been applied for, and Sophia determines to flee. To facilitate this, Honour gets herself turned away. Meanwhile Tom, on his journey, goes to an inn on the way to Bristol. A company of soldiers arrive; there is an argument, and Tom joins them as a volunteer. Ensign Northerton insults Sophia; Tom waxes angry but is felled by a bottle. Northerton is detained, while Tom is treated or perhaps mistreated by the incompetence of the surgeon. Tom is anxious to fight Northerton, is nearly swindled by the sergeant over the price of a sword; then Northerton is helped by the landlady to escape.

Book 8

The fifteen chapters of this book cover two days. The landlady visits Tom and sees that he has little money, tells the surgeon this, whereupon the latter leaves his patient. Jones meets a barber who is called Little Benjamin, but who turns out to be Partridge, the supposed father of Tom. Partridge tells Tom that he is not his father, but agrees to go with him on his expedition. Having paid the landlady, they set out. They arrive at a superior kind of inn in Gloucester; there Tom meets the lawyer Dowling who had brought the news of Mrs Blifil's death (see Book 5). A pettyfogger manages to malign Tom to the landlady, with the result that she offends Tom, who pays his bill and leaves.

Partridge is under the illusion that Tom is going to join the Pretender (Partridge himself is a Jacobite). They arrive at a house, which they enter. Outside, the owner of the house is attacked by ruffians, but is saved by Tom. There follows the Man of the Hill's story about his youthful excesses, this being interrupted by a short story from Partridge. The Man of the Hill rediscovers his father, and meets too his old corrupter, Watson, in his story; he later has a discussion with Tom after revealing that he is a widely travelled man.

Book 9

This short book of seven chapters covers twelve hours. The first chapter is the now familiar author digression, but this quickly passes into the second chapter in which Jones rescues a lady in distress. He finds that her assailant is Ensign Northerton, who escapes. Tom takes the lady to Upton, where they stay at an inn. The state of the lady arouses suspicion, and the landlady and landlord attack Tom; Partridge and the maid also become involved, when a young lady and her maid arrive. They are followed by some soldiers, one of whom recognizes the lady whom Jones has saved as Captain Waters' lady. The latter forgives the landlady, and Tom makes it up with the landlord. Mrs Waters begins to cast languishing eyes upon Tom, Partridge builds up their importance in kitchen conversation, and so much is drunk that the coachman is in no fit state to depart with the young lady who had arrived. The last chapter provides retrospect on Mrs Waters and Ensign Northerton, the latter having been intent on killing the lady and making off with her money and goods when Tom arrived to rescue her.

Book 10

Another short book, here of nine chapters. An Irishman arrives at the inn in the middle of the night. He is in pursuit of his wife, and Susan the maid shows him to Mrs Waters' room. Tom leaps from the bed, a row ensues (yet another), but later the facts are hushed up by Tom saying that hearing a noise he had come into Mrs Waters' room. Another rich lady now arrives. Her servant talks below stairs (having condescended to everybody) and then returns to her lady. It is none other than Mrs Honour and, of course, Sophia is with her. Mrs Honour learns that Tom 'is in bed with a wench', Sophia learns much from the maid Susan, and as a result becomes very upset. Sophia and Honour quit the inn; Tom discovers too late that they have left, and Mr Fitzpatrick, the Irishman, searches fruitlessly for his wife. Suddenly Western arrives in search of his daughter but only just missing Mrs Fitzpatrick, who is his niece. Supple notices that Tom is holding Sophia's muff, Western searches the inn, Mrs Waters is again disturbed, and Western goes off after Sophia. There follows retrospect on Sophia's escape in order to account for her original appearance at the inn in Upton.

Book 11

The events of three days are contained in ten chapters. The first chapter deals trenchantly with critics; then, in the next chapter, plunges into Sophia's journey. To her great joy, she encounters her cousin Mrs Fitzpatrick. She arrives at an inn, where the landlord concludes that she is Jenny Cameron (see note p.82). Sophia decides to go to London; Mrs Fitzpatrick relates her history to Sophia: how her husband had run into debt, and how she had suffered at his hands. Her narrative is broken off while the landlord, still convinced that he is housing Jacobite ladies, tells them that the French have landed. An Irish peer arrives who knows Mrs Fitzpatrick. He sets off with them the next morning (Sophia has lost her money) and they arrive in London, where they take lodgings, Mrs Fitzpatrick being determined to 'cast herself under the protection of some other man'. Sophia realizes this, and goes to stay with Lady Bellaston.

Book 12

Again the same number of days are under focus. Western in hot pursuit of Sophia, is easily side-tracked into a nearby hunt, after which he returns home. Jones and Partridge set out, Tom often distracted by his loss of Sophia. They meet a beggar, who has Sophia's pocket-book and the bank-bill she had lost. They reward the man, who tries to get more from them. Once more they come to an inn, where they watch a puppet show. Jones learns news of Sophia from the Merry-Andrew and from the boy who had conducted her. He sets out, meets Mr Dowling, and relates his history to him. On the way to Coventry they meet a group of gypsies, who demonstrate the integrity of their justice. Jones and Partridge journey on and are nearly robbed when within a mile of Highgate.

Book 13

These twelve chapters cover twelve days. Tom, in London in search of Sophia, arrives at Mrs Fitzpatrick's just after Sophia has left. Mrs Fitzpatrick visits Lady Bellaston, who is intrigued by her description of Tom. She later meets him at Mrs Fitzpatrick's. Meanwhile, Tom, on his way to his lodgings, rescues a gentleman called Nightingale from being beaten up by his footman. Next day he receives an invitation to a masquerade, and borrows money from Partridge in order to go. Nightingale, in love with the landlady's daughter Nancy, accompanies him. Tom is accosted by a lady in a mask, who later turns out to be Lady Bellaston. The latter gives Jones money – he now becomes a kept man – and he generously gives some of it to Mrs Miller, who has just told a very moving story of one of her relatives in distress. Lady Bellaston becomes violently fond of Tom. Mrs Miller's relation comes to thank Tom for saving his family. Tom goes to see Lady Bellaston, and Sophia unexpectedly comes home early from the play. She taxes Tom with having gossiped about her in inns, but the lovers come together, only to be interrupted by the dramatic entrance of Lady Bellaston. The latter talks with Sophia when Tom has gone and indeed torments her about his identity.

Book 14

Ten chapters covering two days of action. Tom is pestered by letters from Lady Bellaston. She visits him but has to be hidden when Mrs Honour appears. Tom gets a letter from Sophia via Mrs Honour, and Mrs Miller criticizes him for having a lady in his room. Nightingale informs Tom that he will be leaving the lodgings; Tom taxes him with having made Mrs Miller's daughter Nancy fall in love with him. Nightingale's father has already made a match for him. Mrs Miller tells Jones the story of her life, and there follows Nightingale's desertion of Nancy. Nightingale reveals that he is not his own master, and Tom undertakes to try to get Nightingale's father on his side. He fails, but apparently gets the uncle's approval of the marriage of his nephew to Nancy Miller. The uncle visits the Millers, but when he learns that Nightingale is not really married to Nancy he says how glad he is; uncle and nephew go off together. Book 14 ends with Mrs Honour's arriving to bring bad news of Sophia.

Book 15

Twelve chapters, 'in which the history advances about two days'. Lady Bellaston encourages a nobleman's interest in Sophia. This Lord Fellemar is already in love with her. Lady Bellaston persuades a friend to tell the lie in front of Sophia that Tom has been killed in a duel. Sophia faints, Lady Bellaston tells her the truth, and Lord Fellemar begins his suit to Sophia. He tries – though not very hard – to force her, when her father bursts in upon them. Parson Supple tries to restrain Squire Western, as does Lady Bellaston, but he carries off Sophia to confinement, Lady Bellaston being secretly pleased, since this leaves her free to keep Tom for herself. We are now brought back to Mrs Honour's visit to Tom. This is interrupted by the arrival of

Lady Bellaston; there is trouble between the two women, but they make it up.

Meanwhile Nightingale's uncle learns that his daughter has disobeyed him and has run off with a parson. Tom receives more letters from Lady Bellaston. He confides in Nightingale, who acquaints him with the lady's true character and advises him to propose marriage to her. She immediately thinks that Tom is after her money, and of course rejects him. Hot-foot upon this comes a letter from Allworthy to Mrs Miller stating that he intends to come up to town and will stay in her lodgings. Nightingale is married to Nancy, Mrs Honour is employed by Lady Bellaston, and another lady, Mrs Hunt, proposes marriage to Tom. He rejects her. Partridge brings the news that he has met Black George and that Sophia is in town to be wed to Blifil, who will be arriving with Allworthy. Tom determines to write to Sophia.

Book 16

Ten chapters, 'containing the space of five days'. Sophia confined in a house in Piccadilly, with Western and the landlord enjoying each other's company. A visitor comes from Lord Fellemar demanding satisfaction for Western's insults to him. There is a further argument. Black George meanwhile smuggles Tom's letter in to Sophia and when she meditates on it that evening she hears the row below. Tom gets a letter from Sophia in which she says she has more liberty. There follows a description of a visit to the theatre to see *Hamlet*, in which 'Partridge afforded great mirth'. Mrs Fitzpatrick approaches Tom and makes an appointment to see him the next day.

Blifil meanwhile persuades Allworthy that he loves Sophia, and this is the occasion of the visit to town. Western and Blifil burst in upon Sophia and her aunt, and Lady Bellaston arranges with Lord Fellemar to have Jones kidnapped and impressed for service. She also sees Mrs Western with a view to having Lord Fellemar marry Sophia. She produces Tom's written proposal of marriage to her. Mrs Fitzpatrick urges Tom to court Miss Western as a cover for his intentions towards Sophia, but Miss Western summons Fitzpatrick to London to find his wife. He meets Tom, they fight, and Fitzpatrick appears to be mortally wounded. Tom is taken away to prison, and gets a letter from Sophia saying that she has seen his letter of proposal to Lady Bellaston.

Book 17

Nine chapters, comprising the action of three days. Blifil reveals Tom's 'crime' to his uncle, but Tom finds a stalwart champion in Mrs Miller. Western tells Allworthy the news of Sophia, and Allworthy withdraws Blifil's suit to her. He later gives him permission to approach Sophia but insists that she must not be confined. Sophia virtually gets permission from her aunt to behave distantly to Felle-mar. Mrs Miller and Nightingale visit Tom in prison, and Mrs Miller goes to see Sophia, to tell her of Tom's goodness. She then warns Allworthy that 'time will show all matters in their true and natural colours'. Meanwhile Blifil and the lawyer Dowling have become very close companions. Lord Fellemar is turned down by Sophia, Miss Western cross-questions Mrs Miller, and then harangues Sophia over receiving a letter from Tom. Tom is made the more miserable by what Nightingale has discovered, but his spirits are lifted by the arrival of Mrs Waters, who tells him that Mr Fitzpatrick is not seriously injured, and that he has admitted he was the aggressor.

Book 18

The final book of thirteen chapters, covering 'about six days'. Partridge tells Jones that Mrs Waters is his (Tom's) mother. Tom is visited by Black George, and later Allworthy visits old Nightingale, questions him about Black George, and finds that he has hoarded the bank bills which Allworthy gave to Tom all that time ago. A letter from Thomas Square saying how he has wronged Tom moves Allworthy; he is unimpressed by a letter from Thwackum, which expresses no surprise at Tom's present state. The attempt to kidnap Tom comes to light, Blifil twists what he actually did, Allworthy then forgives him and sees Partridge. The latter tells him his story, and of course that of Mrs Waters and Tom. Mrs Waters then appears, and is left alone to talk with Allworthy.

She reveals that Tom's father was a clergyman's son called Summer who died young, and that the mother was – Allworthy's sister. Western then arrives with his news that Sophia has been writing to Tom, Mrs Waters continues her story, and Dowling, entering, reveals that Blifil has employed him to make the case black against Tom. He also reveals that Blifil has concealed the death-bed confession of his mother that Tom is her son and thus Allworthy's nephew. Blifil has to endure Allworthy's knowledge of this, for the squire makes it clear to him that he knows the truth. Allworthy then visits Sophia and tells her the news. Western attempts to treat Sophia roughly; Tom is reunited with Allworthy and reconciled to Western, Fellemar having helped in Tom's release. Tom goes to Blifil and finds the latter at first sullen but then spuriously repentant. Allworthy tells Tom of Black George's appropriation of his money. Tom is now aided and abetted by Western in his courtship of Sophia, and all is happiness. Allworthy gives Blifil £200 a year; Square dies; Mrs Fitzpatrick is separated from her husband, and Mrs Waters marries Parson Supple. Partridge marries Molly Seagrim. Tom and Sophia have two children.

Critical commentaries, textual notes and revision questions

Note: all references in the commentaries below are to the Penguin edition of *Tom Jones* edited by R. P. C. Mutter, but since the commentaries and notes follow the sequence of the novel itself, they can be used with any edition of *Tom Jones*.

Dedication

This is to Fielding's friend and patron, George Lyttleton (1709–73). The tone is fulsome but sincere, and the fourth paragraph contains a reference to Fielding's model for the character of Squire Allworthy, Ralph Allen, who also helped the author financially and is said to have cared for his family after his death. The dedication contains some fine examples of Fielding's style, as well as some definite indications of intent, such as 'I declare, that to recommend goodness and innocence hath been my sincere endeavour in this history . . . I have endeavoured strongly to inculcate, that virtue and innocence can scarce ever be injured but by indiscretion.'

Do good by stealth, and blush to find it Fame Pope's praise of Fielding's friend Ralph Allen (see above) in his *Epilogue to the Satires, Dialogue I*, line 136.

Book 1

Chapter 1

The analogy is with eating, an appropriate extended metaphor, since there is much eating at inns during the course of the novel. The author's tone in the introductory chapters to each of the books is one of intimacy, a confiding in the reader of his intention and practice. Fielding's ingenuity in sustaining the metaphor is apparent. Human nature is his subject and, continuing his chosen image, he asserts that his own skill 'in well dressing it up' is what matters. He will begin with plain fare – the country – and then proceed to the 'seasoning of affectation and vice which courts and cities afford'. Note that Fielding keeps to this scheme.

eleemosynary i.e. dependent on charity.
ordinary Tavern.
nice Particular.
particular bills i.e. of fare, menus.
the Alderman of Bristol Aldermen were known for their gluttony. The tortoise is the turtle, much eaten as a delicacy in this period.
calibash and calipee i.e. those edible parts of the turtle which are found under the upper and lower shells.
True wit is nature . . . Pope, *Essay in Criticism*, 297–8.
Heliogabalus the emperor of Rome (218–22 AD) known for his eating and sexual excesses.
ragoo it i.e. make a highly-seasoned stew (ragout) of it.

Chapter 2

Detailed description of Allworthy makes him the possessor of all the virtues and prepares us for his enlightened kindliness in his many good actions. Note the biographical link with Fielding himself – his own wife had died some two years before he began to write *Tom Jones*. There is something touching (and of course deeply religious) in the fact that Allworthy considers his wife to be still with him – as she obviously is in the spirit. Bridget Allworthy is presented ironically, and Fielding himself tells the reader of his favourite form of self-indulgence, which he intends to employ throughout the novel – his digressions.

the age of 30 Later she is said to be nearly forty.
the trained bands armed citizens formed in times of war as a kind of extension of the army. The reference here is an ironic one calling their courage in doubt.
I intend to digress A statement of his practice in *Tom Jones*.
any pitiful critic Fielding often disparages criticism, indicating that critics are frequently incapable of judgement.

Chapter 3

Some irony directed at the conventional representation of character and at certain 'droll authors' who write conventional history. Note the vagueness about Allworthy's absence in London, and the casually dramatic introduction of the foundling into the story. There is neat irony too at the preparations of Mrs Deborah Wilkins to go into the company of her master and some mockery of the reader's expectations of this scene. Mrs Wilkins is coarse, vengeful, and obviously sexually repressed. She is also lacking in Christian charity, since she wants the baby put out in the cold regardless of whether it lives or not.

Allworthy shows his susceptibility, generosity and natural Christian feeling.

offals i.e. leavings.
free-stone i.e. a stone tablet with the benefactor's name and good qualities engraved on it, another compliment by Fielding to the good works of his friend Ralph Allen.
The History of England Fielding had already mocked certain of his contemporaries who had written inaccurate histories, among them Thomas Carte, whose *General History of England* began to appear in 1747.
without Outside.
my graver reader Note the mockery in Fielding's tone.
your warrant Remember that Allworthy is a magistrate.
Bridewel Later spelt Bridewell; a house of correction, after St Bride's Well, in London.
whipt at the cart's tail Under a law of the reign of James I, such punishment for the mother of an illegitimate child was permissible.
hap Chance; here, misfortune.
apter More likely.
strokes i.e. statements, assertions.
pap i.e. bread softened with milk.

Chapter 4

Detailed and elaborate description of Allworthy's house and surroundings, reflecting the 18th-century interest in architecture and landscape gardening as well as giving an account of Fielding's own home at Sharpham Park. Fielding brings us down to earth – and down the hill – by a wonderfully informal invitation. In view of the revelations to come in the plot, we understand Miss Bridget's silence when she sees the baby. Her praise of her brother's charity in caring for it perhaps owes something to her guilt (this is the equivalent of dramatic irony, since only she knows the truth – we, the readers, and Allworthy, are in ignorance).

Gothick The style of architecture prevalent in Western Europe from the 12th to 16th centuries.
winded Archaic usage = wound.
as harbingers preceding his pomp The simile is in the mock-heroic manner characteristic of the novel.
Reader, take care . . . Typical Fielding intimate address to the reader.
complacence i.e. wish to please.
owning Declaring.
an impudent slut . . . The irony is that, in view of what is later revealed, she is calling herself all these names!

appellation Name.
diligence i.e. care, conscientiousness.

Chapter 5

Mrs Wilkins is dependent on the reactions of her mistress: the servant-mistress situation is here shown early (compare Mrs Honour and Sophia later). There is some neat irony ('had it been a child of her own') and again some evidence of guilt and shame, and the determination to cover her own tracks, by her reference to the baby as a 'little brat'. Fielding himself interrupts the narrative to lend his assistance, as he puts it, in explaining the grumbles of Miss Bridget.

all charity is condemned by law as irreligious The law required
  foundlings to be cared for, but Fielding is probably referring to the fact
  that no illegitimate child could inherit property.
humours Whims, moods.

Chapter 6

The mock-epic tone continues with an extended simile, about which the author himself takes a modestly humorous tone. There is certainly evidence of the study of human nature here, with the assertion that those who are servile to their superiors tend to tyrannize 'over little people'. Jenny Jones is liable to provoke jealousy and suspicion anyway because of her learning, but note that she is judged without evidence. Her superiority is calculated to provoke ill-will in her contemporaries, and her new-found capacity to dress well makes things worse. There is a plot-clue in Jenny's attendance at Allworthy's house; her confession, so facile, is another. The chapter ends on a note of expectation, with Jenny about to be interviewed by Allworthy.

Not otherwise than when a kite . . . The parody of the epic simile.
sowered i.e. soured.
a very uncommon share of understanding i.e. she was very intelligent.
quickness of parts Aptitude for learning.
must have a good stomach i.e. must have a strong constitution (to enjoy
  sleeping with someone like Jenny).
House of Correction See note on Bridewel p.26.

Chapter 7

Allworthy reveals his humanity and compassion in his initial address to Jenny. At the same time, he gives her a rather heavy-handed sermon, and dwells on the fact that the woman has degraded herself by yielding to the importunities of the man. Typically, he shows his goodness by offering to get Jenny away to save her from the law and to provide for her child. Jenny shows her own character by her refusal to name the father, the irony being that she is guiltless and that she has the loyalty not to give away Miss Bridget.

bubble i.e. plaything, tool.
the Scripture bids us love our enemies Matthew 5:44.
denounced Pronounced.
obloquy Condemnation.
documents i.e. instructions.

Chapter 8

This reveals something of the character of Miss Bridget, who eaves-drops on her brother's sermon to Jenny, doubtless to see that the latter does not betray her. Deborah again shows her unscrupulousness in wanting to discover the father, and the author indulges in the mock-heroic and in satire against society by his mention of Lady Seraphina. There is irony in Deborah's having to adjust herself to her mistress's view of the case. This hypocrisy Fielding affects to com-mend by calling her an 'able woman, and truly great politician'. Miss Bridget is certainly the greater hypocrite here.

This be . . . O wicked, wicked wall The reference is to the mechanicals' play in *A Midsummer's Night's Dream*, though the actual words are spoken by Pyramus (Act 5, Scene 1).
de non apparentibus . . . What is not seen must be treated as if it does not exist. (A legal maxim.)
Venus . . . the laughter-loving goddess In the *Iliad*, Book 3, line 424.
Tysiphone One of the Furies in Greek mythology.
Boreas The north wind.
consonant In agreement.
forc'd Raped.

Chapter 9

A chapter on human nature in reaction, hence the outcry against Jenny and the tendency to condemn rather than forgive. Naturally rumour now credits Mr Allworthy with being the father of the child, and Jenny comes to be pitied.

beating hemp i.e. the employment of women in a house of correction, but derived here from Hogarth's *The Harlot's Progress*.

impolitic Unwise.

good gossips Ironic – good at spreading gossip.

as it will be some time . . . Note the omniscient voice telling us – up to a point – what will happen.

Chapter 10

A description of the enlightened behaviour of Allworthy within his own house, where there is considerable freedom for its inhabitants to do as they wish. Dr Blifil is represented as being frustrated because of his career, and Allworthy as the kind of man who always befriends misfortune. Blifil is represented as a good man too, and his generosity of spirit – indeed his religious exercise of goodness – is shown in his wishing his brother to marry Miss Bridget.

application to letters i.e. the study of literature, philosophy, history etc.

indigent Poor.

elemosynary See note, p.25.

losing i.e. wasting.

namesake . . . Roman kalendar St Bridget (c.451–523) of Ireland, in the Roman Catholic list of Saints.

indulgencies i.e. practices.

purchased the post Commissions were bought, colonels of regiments being all-powerful. Because he had quarrelled with the colonel, he was obliged to sell his commission, which would obviously in turn be sold by the colonel to someone else.

rusticated Retired to the country.

Methodism Founded by John Wesley (1703–91) and George Whitefield (1714–70); the movement was distrusted by Fielding and frequently mocked by him.

aggrandizing i.e. making them better off financially, etc.

the art of love as Ovid . . . Fielding himself translated and published the Roman poet Ovid's *Art of Love* in 1747.

Chapter 11

The author is ironic about middle-aged people falling in love, about what constitutes handsome appearance and good breeding, and finds time to mock high-society gentlemen and town education. He turns it all into caricature by saying that Hogarth has already taken Miss Bridget's portrait. The mercenary motives of the Captain are given, and in addition the coyness of the lady comes in for a share of the irony. It is noticeable that the Captain fears that Allworthy will withdraw his promise to make any child of Bridget's his heir when he learns of the Captain's proposal. The outward behaviour of the Captain and Bridget to each other is hypocritical.

chairman i.e. the man who carried the sedan-chair, an individual means of transport, with a 'chairman' at each end.

Mr Hogarth . . . a Winter's Morning Hogarth (1697–1764), friend of Fielding and outstanding artist of social scenes of the period, 'Morning' being from *The Four Times of the Day* (1738).

nicety Delicacy.

matrimonial banquet Note the recurrence of the sexual/eating image.

hereditaments i.e. his possessions which would be inherited by his heir.

the Witch of Endor See 1 Samuel, 28,7–25, where Saul consults her.

express Direct.

nolo episcopari 'I do not wish to be made a bishop', the statutory reply made when offered the title.

the citadel was defended in form . . . this is the first of the military images.

Chapter 12

The interesting thing here is that Allworthy is beforehand in the knowledge of what has happened, and this shows the doctor's deception in a poor light. The latter appears to be trying to get on the right side of Allworthy, but this is certainly the wrong way to do it. Allworthy, while noting beauty, speaks forcefully for the Christian principles on which all love should be based.

more averse Less likely.

sui juris Having the full legal capacity to act.

a small discomposure of his muscles i.e. he was laughing at what Allworthy was saying.

Chapter 13

The jealousy of Blifil and his determination to get rid of his brother gives Fielding the opportunity to moralize on the paying back of a friend for what he has done for you by, of course, rejecting him. Consequently the captain treats his brother cruelly, even using his words with Allworthy against him. The chapter reveals the capacity of Allworthy to be duped, since he accepts the superficial reconciliation of the brothers – a character trait, for he is to be duped later. The captain's jealousy of his brother's attainments is also stressed.

I paid you off i.e. I put paid to you.

Revision questions on Book 1

1 Write an essay on Fielding's use of his own voice.

2 Compare and contrast either Allworthy and Captain Blifil *or* Miss Bridget and Deborah Wilkins.

3 Which scene most impresses you so far and why?

4 Indicate the main qualities of Fielding's style so far.

Book 2

Chapter 1

Fielding defines his selective methods, thus explaining the time he gives to particular incidents and phases of the fictional lives of his characters. He attacks those 'histories' that are merely intent on filling up pages regardless of interest. There is some comparison with a lottery, an underlining of fate.

an apology for a life A knock at the poet laureate, Colley Cibber (1671–1757) who had published his autobiography in 1740.
amanuensis Secretary, servant.
Ad confligendum . . . From Lucretius, *De Rerum Natura*, 3, lines 833–7.
Mr Creech (1659–1700) The translation was first published in the 1680s.
the lottery . . . drawn at Guild-hall From 1694–1826 state lotteries were held at the Guildhall to raise money for such projects as the building of Westminster Bridge. There was much profiteering, and the lottery was the subject of a number of satirical attacks by Fielding.
jure divino tyrant A political knock at the King ruling by divine right, and therefore at the Jacobites (see the section on the background to *Tom Jones* on p.12).

Chapter 2

Briefly cutting irony on the fact that Blifil was born eight months after the wedding, i.e. that he was illegitimately conceived, thus providing a natural parallel with Tom. The jealousy and the viciousness of the captain are exposed; they are offset by the genuine Christian charity of Allworthy, and the chapter ends on a note of mystery, with the identity of the father about to be disclosed.

the living monuments of incontinence i.e. they testify to the sexual
indulgence of the parents.
He visits the sins of the fathers . . . the children's teeth . . . on edge . . .
See Exodus, 20,5 and *Ezekiel* 18,2–3.
parabolically i.e. in the form of a parable.

Chapter 3

Retrospect on the schoolmaster and his wife, ironically observed.
Their childlessness is the cause of the wife's jealousy, and the chapter
is made dramatic when this jealousy is unleashed upon Jenny.
Fielding is deliberately reticent when he chooses to be – i.e. over the
sexual enjoyment of Mrs Partridge – but we note that Partridge is
diplomatic in letting Jenny go, and not a little jealous of her himself.

Rules directly contrary to those of Aristotle See *Politics*, 1,5. He says
that the husband is meant to control his wife and his family.
more emolument A higher salary.
Eton and Westminster The two great public schools.
syntaxis Sentence structure in Latin, taught in the lower forms.
the Harlot's Progress See note p.28.
Xantippe The overbearing wife of Socrates.
commemorated i.e. referred to.
Da mihi aliquid potum Poor Latin for 'Give me something to drink.'
the trencher A food container.
full as Just as.
'To make a life of jealousy . . . *Othello* Act 3, Scene 3.
'Leve fit . . . Ovid, *Amores*, 1,2.

Chapter 4

The unreliability of Mrs Partridge stressed, with a build-up to her
changes of mood and a digression (the latter always part of the
Fielding manner), here intent on classical analogies with the present
case. The power of rumour emerges, with a mock-epic simile to
introduce the results. There is a zest and coarseness about the
domestic battle that Fielding enjoys, and a considered appraisal of the
injustice done to Partridge.

Free Masonry Fielding often satirizes the secrecy and concealed practices
of the society.
Nemesis In Greek mythology, the goddess of retribution and vengeance.
descanting i.e. enlarging upon.
barbers news was a proverbial expression i.e. because rumours were
generated there, as mentioned by the Greek writers Plutarch and Lucian,
as well as the Roman Horace.

Horace A reference here to his *Satires*.

the coffee-houses A contemporary reference, for these places were known
  for the gathering of wits, men of fashion, etc.

overseer i.e. of the workhouse.

as fair Grimalkin The mock-epic simile, Grimalkin being the cat.

redundant i.e. larger, longer.

Amazonian A reference to the race of Greek warrior women.

una voce With one voice.

as we are taught that of a murdered person often doth See Genesis,
  4,10.

Chapter 5

Again there is the emphasis on the power of rumour, together with the
cunning of Mrs Wilkins and her foreseeing that Captain Blifil will be
her master. And there is the cunning of the Captain in concealing the
knowledge of Tom's (supposed) fatherhood until he (the Captain)
can use it. He does this with due religious hypocrisy, and once again
the chapter ends with expectation.

that we are liable to be imposed upon Note the irony – the Captain is
  himself imposing upon Allworthy.

epicures . . . predicated . . . largesses Note the high-flown tone of the
  language, which in a sense reflects Allworthy's unworldliness.

Chapter 6

Allworthy's good nature and Christian charity are stressed. The
indictment of Partridge arises from the self-interest of Mrs Wilkins,
and Mrs Partridge confounds the situation by her wilful distortion
and lies. The idea of sending for Jenny shows Allworthy's sense of
justice, but it is ironic that she cannot be traced. Fielding himself takes
great delight in concealing the truth from the reader until he shall
choose to reveal it. The further irony is that it is Mrs Partridge's words
that bring down the wrath on her husband's head. The chapter ends
on the hurried note of Mrs Partridge's death (plot contrivance this)
and further evidence of Allworthy's kindness.

Incontinency i.e. in sexual matters.

dispatch Speed.

viva voce In direct speech.

depose Testify.

if it had been out of doors This reflects the irrationality of Mrs Partridge
  – adultery is the same wherever it occurs.

bullocking She means 'bullying'.

an't If it.

a recruiting-officer A contemporary reference, reminding us of the unsettled times.

discovering i.e. revealing.

an order of bastardy The justices of a parish could order that the parents of an illegitimate child could be made responsible for its upkeep.

to found . . . suspicion To base it on.

who soon after caught the smallpox . . . Note the speed of this, essential to the plot in view of Partridge's later role.

distemper Illness.

country i.e. county.

Chapter 7

The Captain's selfish ambitions, and the resultant marital dishar-mony, are the main themes here. The Captain is revealed as thoroughly selfish, scheming, indifferent to and ultimately hating his wife. Their rooted opposition to each other is shown, and the wife's devotion to Tom is an indication of the real relationship she bears towards him. Note that Allworthy only suspects, but does not know, the truth of the relationship, further evidence of his gullibility, which is to be so much in evidence later. The chapter ends once more on a note of expectation.

a Hoadly Hoadly (1676–1761) was Bishop of Winchester and asserted that religion should be based on sincere belief as distinct from external display of worship.

the moroseness of Aristotle himself Aristotle believed that women were by nature inferior to men.

tenements i.e. property.

almost equally with her own child The irony being, of course, that Tom is also her own child.

to do that which rendered him . . . black comedy hint – Fielding means that Bridget will be delighted at the Captain's death.

Chapter 8

A brilliantly ironic brief chapter in which the Captain, in calculating on the death of Allworthy, himself dies.

luxury i.e. licentiousness.

reversions i.e. property, holdings which come to someone on the death of the owner.

mal-a-propos Inopportune, unfortunate.

Tu secanda marmora . . . Horace's *Odes*, 2,18. Fielding's is a free rendering. C. E. Bennet (Loeb Classical Library) translates it as 'yet thou on the grave's verge dost contract for the cutting of marble slabs and, forgetful of the tomb, dost rear a palace.'

Chapter 9

This is a study in dramatic revelation and the hypocrisy that attends it on Mrs Blifil's account. Her brother is genuinely upset while she goes through the whole gamut of simulated grief. The epitaph is a study in the hypocrisy that death so often reveals: false sentiments and, here, a consummately false account of the Captain's character.

an Epitaph in the true Stile In the Captain's case, Fielding is mocking all such extravagant, insincere praises.
visitant i.e. visitor.
dropping Medicine in the form of drops.
gravel Kidney or bladder stones.
fever on the spirits Hysteria, known as the vapours.
His Parts i.e. abilities.
a tender husband . . . Note the hypocrisy in the details of the Epitaph.

Revision questions on Book 2

1 Write an essay on the difference between what appears and what is real in these chapters.

2 In what ways do you find *Tom Jones* a humorous novel so far? Refer to the text in your answer.

3 Compare and contrast the marriage of the Partridges with the marriage of the Blifils.

4 Write on either (a) Fielding's satire or (b) his ability to create tension or (c) a dramatic scene in these chapters.

Book 3

Chapter 1

A deliberate extension of the principles on which the history is based, with due reference to Mrs Blifil's stages of simulated grief, and the emphasis on the selectivity of the author. The tone towards the reader is an ironic one.

emolument See note p.32.
qualify i.e. prepare.
sorrowful . . . sad . . . serious . . . serenity Note the alliteration,
  reflecting the even flow of simulated grief, conventionally observed.

Chapter 2

Tom's harmless childhood vices are treated with due irony. Blifil's
praised virtues are presented in the same way, so that the reader sees
Tom as normal and Blifil as already sycophantic and unhealthy –
determined to be on the right side in everything. There is increased
irony when Fielding comes to deal with the *'preservers* of the *game'*. He
allows himself to digress, but we are aware of a moral sense of
perspective in this account. Tom shows his obstinacy, his loyalty, his
honour and his courage in refusing to betray Black George. The
flogging of Tom is extreme, and between the lines there is moral
condemnation of it. Allworthy reveals his compassionate nature, and
Thwackum his obdurate and sadistic one.

meum and *tuum* Me and you.
smart Pain.
the Bannians in India Hindu merchants who are strict vegetarians.
Horace tells us *Epistles*, 1,2,27.
spring i.e. raise, cause to fly up.
Thwackum Probably based on Richard Hele (1679–1756), canon of
  Salisbury Cathedral.
flead i.e. flayed, lashed.

Chapter 3

Satirical and ironic account of Square, the philosopher who regards
'all virtue as matter of theory only'. This satire is directed against the
deists and free-thinkers who ignored divine revelation. Thwackum
takes the opposite view, believing in the *'divine power of grace'*. Their
arguments demonstrate the inflexibility of each, the tolerance of
Allworthy, and the fact that both men are intent on getting what they
can out of him.

Plato The great Greek philosopher (427–347 BC).
Aristotle Another great Greek philosopher 384–322 BC. He was also a
  scientist and physician. See note p.34.
Coke upon Lyttleton The commentary (1628) by Sir Edward Coke on Sir
  Thomas Littleton, the accepted authority on the law of real property.

Chapter 4

This opens with a digression, lest readers should misconstrue the author's emphasis in presenting Thwackum and Square. They are revealed as odious because both of them have 'utterly discarded all natural goodness of heart'. The character of Blifil is seen in the lie by omission, the cowardice, the tale-telling that involves Black George. Once more Allworthy shows his compassion and understanding, here by withholding punishment.

men who are warm i.e. care passionately about.
A treacherous friend is the most dangerous enemy Fielding has the
   18th-century rational, balanced, sometimes antithetical turn of phrase.
no man is wise at all hours Pliny, *Natural History*, 7,11,131: 'No one is wise
   all the time.'

Chapter 5

The hypocrisy of Square and Thwackum exposed by their praise of Blifil for his conduct in the previous incident. Allworthy's sense of justice is seen in his punishment of Black George, largely because he has allowed Tom to undergo the punishment on his account. The injustice and sadism is seen in Thwackum, forbidden to punish Tom for this matter, making sure that he flogs him on other counts. Blifil is a sycophantic youth who creeps to Thwackum and to Square, while Tom shows his independence of either.

full of birch Intent on thrashing or caning.
a jolly dog i.e. a brave and good fellow.
address i.e. presence, personality.
the imperfect institution of our public schools This may be an ironic
   comment, but Fielding is also underlining Allworthy's naive expectations
   of the effectiveness of a private, home education.

Chapter 6

The opportunism of Square and Thwackum (and hence of course a stress on their insincerity) with regard to Mrs Blifil. The latter shows her knowledge of human nature, and they show their ignorance and unpleasantness by seeking to ingratiate themselves with her through injuring Tom. Her liking for Tom, as well as showing the latter's sexual attraction as he develops into a young man, also hints at the plot revelation later – Tom is her real son, whereas Blifil is the son of her despised husband.

the vale of years i.e. getting past middle age.
stuff o' th' conscience Iago, in *Othello*, 1,2.
Expressum facit cessare tacitum A legal maxim – that which is
expressed cancels that which is silently thought.
Castigo te non . . . Proverbs, 13,24. He that spareth his rod hates his son
. . .
whipt on i.e. pressed on.
imposed upon i.e. influenced.

Chapter 7

Allworthy, moved by compassion, makes up to Blifil for his sister's
preference for Tom. This affects his judgement. Tom is given some
blame because of the natural wildness of his character. Fielding
greatly praises prudence and circumspection as the protectors of
virtue. Strictly, the whole chapter is in the author's voice, though
Fielding apologizes for acting as chorus.

stage . . . actors Note the image, which fits the mock-tragic note being
struck with regard to Tom.

Chapter 8

The beatings of Tom engender a feeling of vengeance in him. His
noble qualities, his care for others, are seen in his selling the horse to
provide for Black George and his family. The irony embraces
Thwackum and Square who, of course, take opposite attitudes towards Tom's conduct.

smart-money i.e. payment for injuries received in his beatings, the phrase
coming from payments made to wounded soldiers and sailors.
perishing Suffering intensely.

Chapter 9

Blifil's cunning (and prudent conduct with regard to money) stressed.
He once more gives Tom away, thus ensuring that he will be
punished. But the debate again shows how delicate is this balance of
domestic power when Mrs Blifil joins in on Tom's side. Tom's
goodness of heart – and a degree of right-minded cunning too – is
shown in his getting Allworthy to see the actual conditions of Black
George and his family, and thus to relieve their poverty-stricken state.

Tillotson's sermons John Tillotson (1630–94) Archbishop of Canterbury,
whose sermons were very popular.

Chapter 10

Irony at the expense of Thwackum and Square continues, (particularly on account of their lacking mercy); also at the expense of the game laws, for Black George is really caught for what is a minor offence. Blifil's lying in the cause of a spurious justice is again in evidence. Allworthy is thus again put upon. Tom approaches Sophia to get her to intercede for Black George. Elaborate preparation is made for the introduction of Sophia.

sitting in her form i.e. in the shape of her body.
higler Travelling dealer in poultry and any wares he could get hold of.
screening i.e. protecting from legal action.

Revision questions on Book 3

1 Write an essay bringing out the contrast between Thwackum and Square.

2 What qualities, in your opinion, make Tom Jones a sympathetic character?

3 Indicate the part played by Blifil in the action.

4 Show how Allworthy is liable to be taken advantage of and indicate his Christian nature.

5 Write an essay on any incident you consider to be either dramatic or humorous in these chapters.

Book 4

Chapter 1

The author's beautifully ironic, omniscient voice mocks his own practice but also the practice of others. He is really writing about the ornamentation of his own work by similes etc. This is really a deliberate build-up to the introduction of Sophia. Stage comparisons of a humorous and digressive nature are also introduced. He intends to introduce Sophia 'with the utmost solemnity in our power'.

an eminent critic Probably Addison (1672–1719), the pages being used by cooks to provide a lining for pastry dishes.

While – history with her comrade ale . . .' Misquoted from the original
Dunciad of Pope (1728) – 'While happier history with her comrade ale . . .'
the opinion of Butler Samuel Butler (1613–80), the reference being to
Part 1 of his famous poem *Hudibras* (1663).
Hortholthrumbo by Samuel Johnson (1691–1773), not *the* Samuel
Johnson. It was produced at the Haymarket in 1729, and enjoyed a vogue
success.
Homer hath ascribed . . . See *Iliad* 2,1–2.
Mr Lock's blind man John Locke (1632–1704), *An Essay Concerning Human
Understanding* (1690) 3,4,11.
King Pyyrhus In Ambrose Phillips's play *The Distressed Mother* (1712) the
part was played by the actor Barton Booth. Wilks was joint manager of
Drury Lane with Colley Cibber and Booth.
Flora The Roman goddess of flowers.

Chapter 2

The mock-heroic romantic tone adopted, a fine parody of the manner
on its own. Fielding ransacks a repertoire of comparisons on Sophia's
account; poets and painters provide the material, until we meet
Sophia herself. There is a poetic but detailed account of Sophia, and
has the merit of progressing to her nature and her mind.

Boreas . . . Eurus . . . Zephyrus The north, east and west winds.
not even Handel can excel George Frederick Handel (1685–1759), the
celebrated composer, lived in England from 1712 onwards. Fielding
greatly admired him.
Venus de Medicis Discovered in the 17th century, and now in the Uffizi
gallery, Florence.
beauties at Hampton-Court Portraits by the court painter Kneller.
each bright **Churchill** *of the galaxy* The four daughters of the Duke and
Duchess of Marlborough.
the *Kit-cat* The club famous in the first two decades of the eighteenth
century, which was composed of the leading Whig statesmen of the day.
Lord Rochester John Wilmot (1648–80), rake and poet.
Lady Ranelagh Her portrait by Kneller was at Hampton Court.
Duchess of Mazarine She came from France to England in 1676, joined
Charles II's court, and was painted by the court painter, Sir Peter Lely.
Sir John Suckling's . . . Her lips were red . . . Suckling (1609–42) was
the cavalier poet, the poem being 'A Ballad upon a Wedding', 11,61–3.
Dr Donne . . . 'Her pure and eloquent blood . . .' John Donne,
celebrated metaphysical poet (1572–1631) later Dean of St Paul's. The
quotation is from the *Second Anniversarie*, lines 244–6.

Chapter 3

Simple retrospect to bring us up to Sophia's eighteenth year. Note the symbolic naming of the bird, an indication of Sophia's ultimate and immediate preference, and what is revealed of the characters of Tom and Blifil and Sophia. The whole chapter contains the action of the novel in miniature.

flea'd See note p.36.

Chapter 4

Thwackum and Square enter into their usual one-sided theoretical debate on the incident. Western shows his impatience with them and Allworthy his understanding that Blifil had acted 'rather from a generous than unworthy motive'. This again shows his trusting nature. The common sense attitude of Western contrasts effectively with the personal animosities of Square and Thwackum.

the elder or the younger Brutus The elder was reputed to have been the first consul of Rome (about 509 BC), while the younger was the prime mover in the overthrow of Julius Caesar (44 BC).

Deist Rational freethinkers who believed in the laws of nature made by God but rejected the trinity.

the elder of parricide i.e. because he condemned his sons to death. (The usual meaning is 'one who kills his father' but can also refer to the killing of a near relative.)

mew i.e. a contained area where the birds were kept.

ferae naturae Of wild nature, not domestic animals.

nullius in bonis Among the goods of nobody.

Chapter 5

Sophia's preference for Tom and her insight into the selfishness of Blifil are given considered weight, Tom being rather better in breeding and behaviour than others who attend the squire's table. We note that neither Tom nor the squire takes any notice of Sophia's increased 'sprightliness' in Tom's company. There is a delightful moment when Tom wishes to speak to her on a serious subject and, to her suprise, it turns out to be a favour for the gamekeeper. Sophia shows her cunning, getting her father to help by repeatedly playing his favourite music. Tom is praised and blamed by gossip, in this as in other instances, and Square and Thwackum become increasingly jealous of him.

PARVA *leves capiunt animos* Ovid, *Ars Amatoria*, 1,159.
crying roast-meat Foolishly announcing one's good luck.
amiable carriage i.e. the easy way in which she conducted herself.
remarked Noticed.
recovered her confusion i.e. recovered *from* her confusion.
always excepted Took exception to.
Mr Handel See note p.40.
Old Sir Simon the King . . . Tunes variously dated from the sixteenth,
seventeenth and eighteenth centuries.
t'other bout i.e. some more of, other verses.
deputation i.e. his freedom from legal action.
sparks Wild young men.

Chapter 6

This is a defence of Tom, who has morality – not opportunism in the
material sense – as a basis for his character; also an attack on those
heroes of contemporary comedy who have no principles. Tom has
principles – which means that he does right where he can and suffers
when he does wrong. Tom's natural sexual appetites are directed at
Molly Seagrim and he becomes the victim of his own passion and her
forwardness. Even here Tom's naiveté is stressed for, as we shall see,
Molly has other lovers. Tom's morality is such that he cannot either
think of betraying Sophia or of abandoning Molly.

the famous trunk-maker in the playhouse See Addison in *The Spectator*
29 November 1711, where he refers to the man placed in the upper gallery
who banged on the floor, benches etc with his stick in order to convey his
approval of the play being performed.
Congreve well says 'there is no true beauty . . .' from his *The Old
Bachelor* (1693) Act 4, Scene 3. Congreve was the greatest of the
Restoration playwrights.

Chapter 7

Molly has a natural degree of vanity, and Fielding has a natural
tendency to satirize church congregations, which he does through
using a political analogy, and also compares the activities of country
people to those of the court.

dressing and ogling i.e. dressing up and flirting.

Chapter 8

Sophia reveals her naiveté by offering to employ the pregnant Molly.
Again Fielding parodies the epic style, here in the vulgar churchyard

battle as the women set upon Molly. It is ironic, grotesque, with this degrading fight given the epic analogies of gods or fallen angels as in Homer or Milton. The pastoral is also mocked in the choice of names. There is a graphic particularity about the description. There is evidence too of Fielding's zestful enjoyment of the whole thing, and he is indicating his social range. Tom's rescue of Molly is mock knight-errantry as well, but we note that Square sees Molly uncovered, almost as if this is his temptation towards her, their relationship developing later until discovered by Tom.

Hudibrass and Trulla Butler's *Hudibras*, 1,3,769 onwards.
starved . . . Butler Sàmuel Butler, though he had a pension, was thought to have starved to death in poverty.
All things are not in the power of all Virgil, *Eclogues*, 8,63.
As a vast herd of cows . . . The epic simile begins the burlesque of Homer's *Iliad*, Books 4 and 5.
pattins wooden shoes.
nor he alone . . . lovely coarse humour implying her licentiousness.
by its horns i.e. he was cuckolded by her.
talents (or rather talons) Note the half-punning wit.
clout Piece of cloth, here head-covering.
Don Quixote The hero of Cervantes' (1547–1616) novel of that name which satirizes chivalric romances. Fielding greatly admired Cervantes and imitated his method in *Joseph Andrews*.

Chapter 9

Fielding is particularly good at domestic scenes, and this one is no exception, a coarse family quarrel to succeed the public one. We also note the change of attitude which ready money brings about, so that Fielding is making his own moral comment here. Violence within the family acts as the great silencer; another comment of a moral and social nature. The chapter ends on a fateful note.

tauked Talked.
voke Folk. Molly's sisters pronounce words beginning with 'f' as though with a 'v'.
a small switch i.e. cane, probably a shoot or branch.

Chapter 10

Supple is made the agent of conveying the news to Sophia after dinner of the churchyard battle and Molly's state – Fielding's irony operates here through Western, who thought that Supple might have news of real importance concerning the nation. Western's immediate conclusion that Tom fathered the child is compounded by his lies over Allworthy. Sophia's own withdrawal is conveniently put down to modesty; she is obviously upset.

battery i.e. her beauty and charm.
Rara avis . . . Juvenal, *Satires*, 6,165.
braken i.e. broken.
her mittimus A warrant to confine her to prison.
smoke it i.e. I know what it is.
therefore i.e. the same thing, fathered a child.
animadvert a pedantic word meaning 'enlarge upon'.
Ingenui vultus . . . Juvenal, *Satires*, 11,154.
errant i.e. complete; later spelt 'arrant'.

Chapter 11

Some satire against the law, even a small criticism of Mr Allworthy's decision in the case of Molly. Tom's conscience and integrity are again in evidence, but when Allworthy reads him a lecture Fielding mocks his own method by sparing the reader, since it is the same one he read Jenny Jones. Allworthy recognizes the 'honour and honesty' in Tom, but Tom's situation is undermined by the hatred of Square, who suggests (and we later learn what his motive is) that Tom had supported the family in order to corrupt the daughter.

in foro conscientiae (Lat.) in a court of conscience.
mittimus See note above.
rhodomontade Bragging.
As Sir Richard Steele says . . . In his play *The Conscious Lovers* (1722), Act 5, Scene 3.
quadrate Square.

Chapter 12

The gossipy nature of Mrs Honour is revealed – she hardly draws breath – and she reveals her interest in Tom. Human nature is certainly displayed in the reactions of Sophia, who talks herself into indifference for Tom, or so she believes. There is the usual digression by the author. Sophia is no longer happy, but the chapter ends again with a mention of Fortune, the prelude to Fate.

Mrs Honour Mrs is a title indiscriminately applied to married and unmarried ladies, generally of mature years.

draggle-tails sluts.
nauseous physic foul-tasting medicine.

Chapter 13

Sophia thinks generously of her father, trying to stop him from being too impetuous. She thinks that she has overcome her feelings for Tom, but of course fortune, in the form of her fall into his arms thwarts her, and compounds this by making her tender towards Tom when she sees that his arm is broken. Fielding employs digression to underline the effect upon Sophia.

Francis Osborne (1592–1659) A misogynist.
Aristotle . . . See *Politics*, 1,5,8.
Bayle Pierre Bayle (1647–1706) French philosopher. The article is, in fact, about the Duke of Guise.
his Odyssey i.e. Homer's, the heroine being Penelope.

Chapter 14

Another satire on the medical profession, at first in the surgeon's treatment of Sophia and then in the torture Tom has to endure. Sophia has to endure Mrs Honour's praise of Tom, which that waiting-woman cunningly observes as she watches her face in the looking-glass. She is cunning enough, too, to back-track when she is accused of being in love with Tom herself. The plot symbol, the muff, with its sexual connotations, is introduced. This, as Honour knows this string of lies will, puts her in good relations with Sophia.

hartshorn The scrapings of deers' antlers, which, in a water solution, was thought to restore the spirits.
blooded i.e. blood drawn off, which was thought to improve the circulation.
miscarried i.e. died.
like Patience on a monument . . . *Twelfth Night*, Act 2, Scene 4: Viola to Orsino on her 'sister's' love.
magnimity a malapropism for magnanimity (generosity of spirit), but what Honour really meant was bravery.
thof Though.

Revision questions on Book 4

1 Write a character study of Sophia Western as she appears in these chapters.

2 What literary devices does Fielding employ in order to sustain his mock-heroic narrative?

3 In what ways is Tom a moral character? You should refer to the text in your answer.

4 Give an account of the role played by Molly Seagrim in the events described in these chapters.

5 Write an essay on the most humorous or most dramatic incident described in these chapters.

Book 5

Chapter 1

The author underlines his own method of prefacing each book of his history with a serious essay. He attacks the various rules of writing, and makes it clear that he is establishing his own. The attack is on the bias of critics – 'The critic, rightly considered, is no more than a clerk' – and stresses that his own method will involve much contrast, and instances the pantomime as a good example of this.

unity of time and place i.e. two of three classical rules for the drama, the third being that of action.

dramatick poetry i.e. plays.

Cuicunque in arte... Each skilful person is to be trusted in his profession.

ipse dixit He himself said it.

at Bath particularly At this time, Bath – because of the waters and fashionable society – would be second only to London as a place to be visited.

the finest brilliant... i.e. the best jewel requires one of less worth to offset it.

Inventas, qui vitam excoluere per artes Fielding provides the translation, the sentence coming from Virgil's *Aeneid*, Book 6,663.

the inventor... the English pantomime John Rich, manager of Covent Garden from 1732 onwards, popularized the pantomime.

Indignor quandoque... From Horace, *Ars Poetica*, lines 359–60.

Oldmixon John Oldmixon (1673–1742), referred to by Pope in *The Dunciad* stressing his dullness.

Sleepless himself... Quotation from *The Dunciad*, 1,93–4.

Chapter 2

Allworthy, though kind, seeks to improve the occasion by taxing Tom
with his past misdemeanours, telling him in effect now that he is over
them to make a new start. The contrasting lectures of Square and
Thwackum are each redolent of their lack of humanity, though
Square biting his tongue provides some humour. Blifil, of course,
stays away, and Western is overpoweringly always there. Tom is
hardly aware of his own feelings for Sophia, but she is palpably moved
by hers for him.

reprobacy i.e. criminal behaviour.
liberavi animam meam I have delivered my soul.
Tully's *Tusculan Questions* Cicero (106–43 BC). In this he discusses the
  question of whether pain is an evil.
Lord Shaftesbury (1671–1713) who believed in natural goodness.
Solomon speaks against Evil Communication Fielding is wrong. See 1
  Corinthians, 15,33.
panacea Cure.
gu . . . zet Go . . . set.
unt had his petticoats on If he hadn't been dressed as he is.
lent un a flick Given him a stroke (with my whip).
the Chevalier Named after the pretender, who was known as the
  Chevalier de St Georges.

Chapter 3

Tom's self-doubts with regard to Sophia's feelings are examined and
his common sense about his own relationship to Western is evident.
His sensitivity is revealed in his pondering, too, on offending
Allworthy, and his fears of what would happen to Molly if he should
desert her.

not as a cold . . . advocate i.e. not from self-interest.

Chapter 4

Fate manifests itself through the gossip of Mrs Honour. Once again
the muff becomes the sexual symbol or, as far as Tom is concerned
here, the romantic symbol of Sophia's love for him. The squire's
throwing the muff into the fire is seen by Tom as confirmation of
Honour's story. Tom sees in Sophia's retrieving the muff her love for
him.

Socrates The Greek philosopher, immortalized in the works of Plato.
Bridewell See note p.26.
the hearing on't i.e. get to know of it.
he bid him beat abroad . . . Naturally the squire uses a hunting metaphor
– here he is telling Tom to get up and not take advantage of just being
there (the squire thinks he has perhaps made overtures to Mrs Honour).
and put her out Interfered with her playing.
Thus the poet . . . Troy Virgil, *Aeneid*, 2,196–8, translated by Dryden
(1631–1700).

Chapter 5

Tom's reactions over Molly further explored, indicating just how
moral he is but also how wrong-headed in thinking that she cares only
for him. His idea of giving her money shows some chink in his moral
armour. There follows one of the funniest scenes in the novel, with
Molly's righteous indignation exposed as hypocrisy, with the revelation of Square in his ridiculous posture of inept concealment. The
whole is enhanced by the detail in the description. Fielding reverts to
the analogy of the meal in order to explain Square's appetite. Notice
the money motif which Molly is understandably intent upon, and
notice Tom's healthy and humorous reaction of laughter to the scene.

egregious Flagrant
transports Expressions of rapture.
liquorish Lecherous, licentious.
which helps off a town lady . . . Fielding is always mocking the town,
where vices are sophisticated.
like Mr Constant in the play The play is *The Provoked Wife*, by Sir John
Vanbrugh (1697) Act 5, Scene 6.
to put his horns i.e. being cuckolded.
KALON The beauty of the mind, the ideal good, from the Greek.
nostrum Medicine – here ironically, since a sum of money is given.

Chapter 6

Tom still continues to blame himself over Molly, an indication of his
sensitivity. He is naturally eased when he discovers the truth that Will
Barnes is the father of the child. Tom's inner conflict over Sophia
shows the advanced stage of his moral sense, and Sophia notices the
change in him. Sophia shows very clearly her capacity for sympathetic understanding of Tom. When they meet by accident Tom
indulges his romantic melancholy at the hopelessness of his position.

trophies i.e. seductions, leading to illegitimate children.
like Free Masons See note p.32 for Fielding's earlier jibe at them.
the famous Spartan theft Plutarch in his *Life of Lycurgus* tells the story of
  the Spartan boy who stole a fox and concealed it under his garments,
  letting it tear out his bowels rather than reveal that he had stolen it.

Chapter 7

The effects of neglecting illness are shown in Allworthy, but not before
a typical Fielding digression on doctors. Allworthy's bravery is
apparent, in view of the physician's telling him he will die, but we are
again forced to question medical unreliability. The interesting thing
here is the generosity of Allworthy in his will, and the natural
outpouring of Tom.

Aesculapian art From Aesculapius, Roman god of medicine.
Venienti occurrite morbo See Persius (AD 34–63), *Satires*, 3,64.
like a French army A contemporary reference, the success of the French
  army in the War of the Austrian Succession (1740–48) enhanced their
  reputation.
Doctor Misaubin French physician who was ridiculed because of his
  obstinate belief in the efficacy of his pills.
Bygar By God.
Cato . . . Let guilt or fear Addison's *Cato* (1713), Act 5, Scene 1.
One of the Roman poets . . . Probably a reference to Lucretius, *De Rerum
  Natura*, 3,938–9.
in specie Money in coins.

Chapter 8

The reactions to the legacies display the selfishness of human nature –
Mrs Wilkins's soliloquy, the debate of Thwackum and Square and the
argument between them. The news of Mrs Blifil's death is important
to the plot, because of the later revelations. Blifil's motive in telling
Allworthy the news is intended to kill his uncle off, and when this fails
the motive for his tears is apparent. We note the Christian resignation
of Allworthy and, as we should expect, the doctor has been wrong
about his being nearly dead.

mourning i.e. mourning clothes.
put in a lump i.e. treated in the same way.
arrow a servant Not one.
St Paul hath taught me . . . Philippians, 4,11.
How . . . above stairs Fielding is mocking the tone of the doctor enquiring
  about his patient.

intermit Abate.
Si nullus erit . . . Ovid, *Ars Amatoria* 1,151. (Fielding gives the translation.)

Chapter 9

Tom's loyalty and concern for his uncle, and his justifiable anger at Blifil's telling him the news. This is followed by Tom's natural excesses in celebration of Allworthy's recovery, an important incident that is going to be distorted and held against him in the future. There is a digression on the effects of drink, which merely releases the tendencies we already have. On the cessation of this the quarrel between Tom and Blifil ensues, which causes worse feelings against Tom to be stored up for later use. Square now knows his position, and maintains his neutrality.

Aeschines Celebrated Greek orator.
throwing in the bark By prescribing quinine, obtained from the bark of the Cinchona tree.
bumpers Heavy drinking – glasses filled to the brim, then more.
Quis, desiderio sit pudor Horace *Odes*, 24,1–2.
in *statu quo* i.e. back to normal.

Chapter 10

Tom walking in the grove naturally thinks of Sophia now that he is free from the immediate worry of Allworthy. On meeting Molly, however, he gives way to his sexual inclinations. Fielding explains this by saying that wine ruled him, and then undertakes another digression about this. Action is the keynote of this chapter, and we note that even here Blifil lies to Square by not revealing that he has seen Tom with a wench, knowing that the discovery will be the more effective.

sweet trilling . . . nightingales Fielding is here parodying the artificial language of much 18th-century poetry.
Circassian i.e. a native of Circassia, on the shores of the Black Sea.
Grand Signior's seraglio i.e. the Sultan of Turkey's harem.
parly Discussion.
the laws of Pittacus Aristotle, *Politics* 2,9,9.
retired with his Dido Fielding is following the *Aeneid*, Book 4,165–6 where Aeneas and Dido shelter from the rain, Blifil being substituted for Dido.
fired at i.e. became angry.
found sitting i.e. like a bird.

Chapter 11

Much coarse innuendo in this chapter. Like the previous fight, this one is described with much zest – we feel that Fielding delights in these coarse scenes, and we share the delight. The action is added to by the arrival of Western – and this is a good example of Fielding's graphic narration.

Mr Pope's period of a mile This is Pope versifying John Donne in a satire (1733) and attacking the long-windedness of Bishop Hoadly.
Rutting The season for stag-rutting is mid-September–mid-November.
Venus Ferina Suggesting a love goddess of wild animals, i.e. their mating.
Samean mysteries Samos, an island sacred to Juno, who ruled over marriage and childbirth.
ferine Wild.
Virgil . . . -*Procul, O procul* . . . *Aeneid*, 6,258–9, trans. Dryden.
genus omne animantium The whole race of human creatures.

Chapter 12

A spectacle – Fielding paints a mock-epic picture of those on the battlefield. Sophia faints, thus arousing dramatic interest, and Tom restores her, gives her a caress, thus occasioning the author's light irony. Notice the further irony of the fact that Jones is at this stage a hero to Western. The next digression is humanitarian in tone: Fielding, doubtless with contemporary hostilities in mind, wishes that wars could be settled by bloody heads and noses rather than 'mangled and murdered human bodies'. Western shows his coarseness and his delight that Tom has had a wench, but Sophia suffers from his words and implications.

King Porus In Plutarch's *Life of Alexander* the latter's victory over the Indian king Porus (326 BC) is described.
the plains of Arcadia The idealized rural setting in Greek mythology.
D'off thy quoat Take your coat off.
feace Face.
att It is (or, you are).
shat Shall.
we'l zee We shall see.
like Mr Bayes's troops From the Duke of Buckingham's *The Rehearsal* (1671), a send-up of the heroic drama.
liquorish See note p.48.
the recruiting . . . numbers i.e. by begetting more children; a contemporary reference to the War of the Austrian Succession (1740–48) in which we fought against France, Spain and Prussia (until 1745) and Bavaria.

Revision questions on Book 5

1 In what ways do you think the first chapter in this section is important to our understanding of Fielding's art in *Tom Jones*?

2 Indicate the part played by Square and Thwackum in these events.

3 In what ways do you think that Fielding is a coarse writer? In your answer, you should refer closely to particular incidents.

4 For whom do you feel the most pity, Tom or Sophia? Give reasons for your answer.

5 Consider the parts played by Mr Allworthy and Blifil in these chapters, and indicate their importance to the plot.

Book 6

Chapter 1

The distinction between love and lust is clearly made. Fielding's intention is to treat of the effects of love, and once more the reader is engaged head-on by the author.

the late Dr Swift The author of *Gulliver's Travels*, who died in 1745.
finders of gold i.e. latrine cleaners (a slang expression).
jakes Latrines.
put the world . . . person Benedick in *Much Ado About Nothing*, Act 2, Scene 1, where he says that it is the 'disposition of Beatrice that puts the world into her person.'

Chapter 2

Note the happiness of Sophia in her silence and Tom in his love, though Sophia is grave as she ponders. Western has little or no discernment, but his sister, who is splendidly caricatured by Fielding, is masculine to look at, is well-read and skilled at politics, is inquisitive, particularly discerning when it comes to the love affairs of other people. The irony plays over her error with regard to Blifil, but though Western believes that 'petticoats should not meddle' he is convinced by her arguments.

Rapin's *History of England*... Rapin (1661–1725) a Huguenot, came to
England in 1788; Eachard – or Echard – (1630–1730) was an unreliable
historian. Many memoirs in French were published at the time.

they belong to us Western is what would today be called chauvinistic.

London Evening-Post Opposition paper satirized by Fielding; it was
founded in 1727.

tan Then.

half the letters are left out i.e. in order to avoid actions for libel.

flick See note p.47

themmun i.e. all these.

King Alcinous . . . Ulysses See *Odyssey*, Book 7,395–402, though the
implication is inaccurate.

plenipo A delegate having the power to act, more commonly called a
plenipotentiary.

Machiavel Machiavelli (1469–1527) the Florentine statesman, author of
The Prince (1513), a treatise on power.

Croat . . . the army of the Empress Queen The reference is to
Maria-Theresa (1717–80), the ruler of the Austrian Empire whose
Croatian troops were employed against Frederick (the Great) of Prussia in
Bohemia in the 1740s.

keep your leagues Honour your treaties.

Chapter 3

This chapter is ironic in the extreme as Sophia seeks to conceal her
feelings for Tom by talking to Blifil, an action calculated to confirm
her aunt's suspicions. This occasions a digression from the author as
well as a satirical snipe at sophisticated society. Allworthy is understandably cautious; also tolerant with regard to marriage, intent upon
not forcing any situation.

discharged out of the custody of physic Note the ironic imprisonment
image – meaning he was freed from the doctor's care.

countermine i.e. effectively get the better of.

bubble Dupe.

Mr Hogarth's poor poet In his *The Distressed Poet*, revised in 1740.

while he well lashes his back i.e. tests his own powers of endurance in the
name of his faith.

Chapter 4

The limitations of Blifil with regard to normal feelings are exposed;
his ability to calculate is stressed. His natural coldness rather upsets
Allworthy, but he is satisfied by Blifil, who manages to conceal his
lack of feeling by Christian professions.

the *Gazette* Founded in 1666, it was the official government paper, giving
court news and appointments.

Chapter 5

There is a satirical treatment of the tears shed over romances to begin
with, and the ironic overplay to the point where neither Sophia nor
her aunt understands what the other is getting at during the first part
of their conversation. The mistaken identity leads of course to climax
and revelation. It also leads to the blackmail of Sophia.

as the French are with our motions i.e. the implication is that the French
government – and army – are one too many for the British.

Chapter 6

We immediately register the opportunist acting of Mrs Honour, who
has been listening at the keyhole. Fielding wonderfully captures the
undisciplined outflow of Mrs Honour, and better still the reaction of
Sophia when she realizes where Jones is. Sophia here dissembles, but
her small vanity of changing the ribbons means that she is too late to
see Tom.

preamble She means, of course, argument.

Chapter 7

Sophia's courage in the face of the visit from Blifil, which is a test of
her endurance. He is a very conceited young man, and we note his
blindness with regard to Tom and the latter's love for Sophia as well
as his motives. The irony continues with the misleading of Western
and the generosity he shows to Sophia, believing that she has accepted
Blifil. There follows the terrible scene in which Western condemns
and threatens her. Tom here acts opportunely, though we feel the
blindness of the squire with regard to him.

un Him.
antic Strange, grotesque.

Chapter 8

The pathetic scene in which the young lovers reveal the noble and
self-sacrificing nature of their love for each other. It is all the more
effective for being almost completely in dialogue.

doated Doted.

Chapter 9

The crisis provoked by Mrs Western's breaking of her word to Sophia and revealing that the latter loves Jones. A mock-epic simile and a contemporary one are employed as prelude. Anti-climax – if such it can be called – confronts the squire when he sees that Sophia has fainted. Western is naturally and provocatively violent and coarse, and Parson Supple's lecture is totally inappropriate. But he knows that he must keep on the right side of the squire.

Strephon and Phillis Names of shepherds and shepherdesses in classical, pastoral love poetry.
the pale livery of death . . . Notice the deliberately artificial language.
the great Dowdy A man in Salisbury who pretended to be a ghost and played practical jokes on strangers.
At unt If you are.
a— Arse.
Seneca In his *Moral Essays*, 3.
Alexander and Clytus Plutarch's *Life of Alexander*, where the latter kills his friend Clytus, who had insulted him during an argument.
my commonplace i.e. my commonplace book, notebook.

Chapter 10

Allworthy rightly points out that Western has brought the whole matter about by putting Tom in Sophia's company so often. Western shows from his conversation just how gullible he is. Blifil distorts as usual for his own ends, and the story of Tom being drunk and having Molly Seagrim have been cunningly kept in reserve until the opportune moment, in order to influence Allworthy strongly against Tom.

with meat for his master i.e. what has been set aside for Blifil.
one smock shall be her portion i.e. one dress will be her dowry.
the *zinking* fund The Sinking Fund was set up by Walpole in 1717 to pay the national debts, but after 1742 it was used to maintain the Hanoverian troops.
a hare sitting i.e. so that it could be caught or killed.
the skin o'er i.e. all he'll get is her person (and not her money).
the Gelding's Plate A race for horses which had been gelded (neutered).
he yet converses i.e. has sexual relations with.

Chapter 11

Allworthy's condemnation of Tom on the evidence of Blifil and Thwackum shows that that good man can be guilty of error. Tom's sufferings rouse the reader's sympathy on his behalf, as they do in his neighbours. The irony of the deception of Allworthy makes for pathos.

Chapter 12

The sufferings of Tom and his struggle with himself over Sophia are poignantly rendered. Fielding now employs the use of the letter to convey feelings and information, a technique that is the staple diet of his great contemporary Richardson. The loss of Tom's pocket-book is important to the plot and to the character of Black George. Here we see earthy hypocrisy in action, in a sense complementary to Blifil's more sophisticated usage. Sophia's letter reveals her genuine concern for Tom.

the gigantic poet Lee A satirical reference to Nathaniel Lee (1653–92) and his high-flown drama *Theodosius: or The Force of Love* (1680).
wafer A moistened leaf of paste used to seal letters.
billet Letter.

Chapter 13

The treatment of Sophia is seen to be cruel, but she has the spirit and ingenuity to resort to pen and paper. The use of terms like 'prison' and 'gaoler' are appropriate to her state. Sophia is also human in her reactions to Tom's giving her up, and Honour overreacts in such a way as to give her mistress more suffering. The gift from Sophia puts Black George in a quandary, but in delivering the money to Tom he is of course concealing the large amount he has found in Tom's pocket-book.

no avocation i.e. nothing to do away from it.
perfidy Malapropism for 'perfidious'.
arrow See note p.49.

Chapter 14

Mrs Western and her argument with the Squire – a demonstration of the power of her reason, a display of the Squire's ignorance and prejudices, and the psychology of Mrs Western, the whole leading to the release of Sophia.

I'd lend him a douse i.e. I'd give him a blow.
Roundheads and Hanover rats Western is a Tory, the Roundheads would be associated with the Whigs, while the Hanover rats reference would be Jacobite condemnation of the King and his troops.

turneps Hanover was portrayed as a turnip garden in the current satires.
the country interest i.e. those Tories who opposed the Pelham
  administration formed in 1744. Fielding despised them.

Revision questions on Book 6

1 Indicate the part played by Mrs Western in these chapters.

2 In what ways do you find the scenes between Tom and Sophia
pathetic? You should refer closely to the text in your answer.

3 Compare and contrast the humour evident in the presentation of
Squire Western and Mrs Honour.

4 Which do you consider to be the most unpleasant scene in these
chapters and why?

5 Consider the part played by deception in this Book.

Book 7

Chapter 1

An investigation of the comparison between the world and the stage,
but with an emphasis here on the audience as distinct from the play
and the actors. The different responses of the various classes of reader
(theatre audience) are described in relation to Black George's theft.
This is the occasion for a digression on human nature as seen in the
fact that the blackest or the lowest condemn those traits in others.

Thespis Horace, *Ars Poetica*, 275–7. Thespis is regarded as the founder of
  Greek tragedy.
St James . . . Drury Lane i.e. the Court rather than the theatre.
Aristotle calls it . . . *Poetics*, 1,2,25,2.
Life's a poor player . . . *Macbeth*, Act 5, Scene 5.
the DEITY By Samuel Boyse (1708–49); the poem went into a second
  edition as a result of Fielding's praise.
similitude Comparison.
Theatre-Royal In Drury Lane.
cloven-footed gentleman Satan, the Devil.
Garrick David Garrick (1717–79) the leading actor of the day.
Scipio the Great . . . Laelius the Wise The first c. 185–129 BC; the
  second his friend, born c. 186 BC.
Horace *Satires* 2,1,71–4.

Cicero In *De Oratore*, 2,6.
Reason the Patentee The latter was the person who was given sole right
 by the Crown to produce plays at a certain theatre.
nil admirari Horace, *Epistles* 1,6,1.
Mr William Mills He died in 1750, Fielding regarding him as a good man
 but an indifferent actor.

Chapter 2

Blifil's cold, contemptuous and unctuous letter causes mixed reactions in Tom, and he indulges his grief at the thought of abandoning
Sophia. He determines to go to sea, but Tom is nothing if not
impetuous, and we doubt his keeping to this.

The world . . . lay all before him *Paradise Lost* 12,646–7: 'The world
was all before them where to choose'.

Chapter 3

The mercenary sermon of Mrs Western to Sophia, followed by an
indication of that lady's ignorance with regard to Socrates' views.
With regard to Sophia's situation, Mrs Western uses the political
jargon with which her vocabulary is imbued. She puts down Sophia –
it is a measure of her obstinacy and ignorance – for having 'inclinations'.

Alcibiades (c. 450 BC) Athenian politician and soldier.
a separate league . . . interest of the Dutch France invaded Flanders in
 1747, but until then the Dutch had been trying to negotiate a separate
 peace with them.
Bailey's *Dictionary* by Nathaniel Bailey, and published in 1721.
bum trap Term of contempt for a bailiff.
shatunt You will not.
You have made a Whig of the girl i.e. put her in opposition to us
 (Western is a Tory).
what Plato says on that subject? The argument is that children who
 disobey their parents in this question of marriage do so at the risk of being
 disowned and disinherited.
that have eat up the nation i.e. because of the cost of the troops.
f—t Fart.

Chapter 4

There is an ironic account of Squire Western's marriage, his wife
being a 'faithful upper servant'. The coarseness and the fact that she

had been married against her will but to her financial advantage are made quite clear, as is the fact that she was the victim – as Sophia could so easily be – of an arranged marriage. The sadistic streak in the Squire makes him delight to run down her mother before Sophia.

whipt in . . . hard run . . . run down Hunting jargon meaning driven hard, the slip, the track, taken or overcome.

King over the Water The Jacobite toast to the Old Pretender, who was exiled in France.

she had been married against her will Western's obstinacy is shown by the fact that his own marital unhappiness is likely to be repeated by Sophia's.

Chapter 5

Sophia uses her own small cunning here to effect a reconciliation between her father and her aunt by the simple expedient of telling him that her aunt intends to leave him her money. Money being the major motivation in his life he blames Sophia for instigating quarrels between him and his sister, and Mrs Honour continues to upset Sophia by her non-stop tactless talking.

lingo of the eyes i.e. 'speaking looks'.

'dite i.e. indict.

College of Chambermaids A finely ironic invention.

Chapter 6

Naturally the result of the reconciliation between brother and sister is a further condemnation of Sophia. The latter has to endure another visit from Blifil, and the eavesdropping shows how unscrupulous the Squire is. The promise of the Squire to Blifil that he shall have Sophia satisfies him because he will have got the better of Tom. Blifil takes delight as ever in maligning Tom. The preparations for the marriage are completed, including the legal settlements, but the end of the chapter makes us feel that it will be forestalled.

placable i.e. easily placated.

war . . . treaty The now familiar imagery, which reflects the situation of the great powers in the world outside.

a rule of Horace *Ars Poetica*, 149–150.

her confident Confidant: to have confided her love for Tom to him.

run in, run in . . . honeys Hunting jargon, perhaps equivalent to 'go after it, my beauties'.

ortolan Bird much valued for its flavour.
preserved a salvo for his conscience i.e. he kept quiet.
previous to the office of the priest i.e. apart from the religious/church
  arrangements.

Chapter 7

Despite all Honour's repetitious ramblings, she manages to convey
the dramatic news of the impending licence to Sophia; the time she
takes contributes to the tension. The atmosphere is dramatic, Sophia
is impetuous and innocent, Honour much more cautious – she knows
more of the world – and also apprehensive about committing herself.
But money, as always in *Tom Jones*, talks, and at the offer of reward
Honour is prepared to risk her virtue. She also cunningly conceives
the plan to get herself turned away, so that she will escape suspicion.

lud Lord.
that to be denied Christian burial . . . Suicides were traditionally buried
  at the crossroads.
lieverer i.e. would rather.
Robin The servant or groom.
after a fiddle i.e. a dance.
one's virtue . . . our livelihood Honour sometimes coins the telling
  phrase – this one is masterly, for a pregnant servant would of course be
  turned away.

Chapter 8

Honour in debate with herself and the temptation to make a greater
profit by confiding all to Western. Greed, one of the major themes of
the novel, is set against fate, the affected superiority of Mrs Western's
maid towards her. There is some fine psychology on age and position
in the argument, with Mrs Western's ugliness a focal point. Honour's
wish to be discharged is effectively brought about.

Quivedo The Spanish satirist (1580–1645).
too upright a judge to decree . . . i.e. too fair to come down on one side –
  irony.
one of the furies Roman name for the Greek Erinyes, the three
  mythological goddesses of vengeance.

Chapter 9

The obstinacy of Mrs Western with regard to Honour, and the slack
nature of Western's administration of the law (he is both biased and

incompetent) are stressed. Fortune favours Honour, who is not sent to Bridewell, and Sophia, who is given a large bank-bill for pretending to fall in with her father's wishes. Fielding makes it clear that while Sophia wishes to show her father all filial love, she succumbs to the thought that she may eventually get Tom.

Bridewell See note p.26.
remitted overlooked, forgiven.
post-chaise Carriage.
to the game i.e. the laws regarding game.
two informations exhibited against him in the King's bench i.e. he had been accused of abusing his authority, of not implementing the law correctly.
the resignation of places of a much greater importance i.e. at court, or in the government.
that strange . . . creature Man The second line of Rochester's *Satire Against Mankind* (1679).
politic sophistry Cunning and deceptive arguments.
Cupid The God of Love.
Punchinello The Italian name from which Punch, introduced in this country after the Restoration, derives.

Chapter 10

A satire against rustic ignorance opens this chapter, with Tom confused by the non-advice he gets. The curious parallel of the Quaker's story about his daughter with Tom's own state is a kind of black comedy, particularly when the Quaker comes to thoughts of revenge. The Quaker's compassion for Tom disappears when he realizes that he is not the gentleman he thought him to be. There is an atmosphere of unease, conveyed by the suspicions of Tom.

gu Go.
honest Broadbrim A reference to the shape of the Quaker's hat.
not fixed to the freehold i.e. which did not go with the house – they have removed all portable goods.

Chapter 11

Graphic narrative of the arrival of the soldiers, the atmosphere aggressive and almost violent until Tom says he will pay the reckoning. There is immediate contemporary reference to the Jacobite rebellion in the mention of the Duke of Cumberland. We note that the guide tries to gain more money, and that the sergeant's boasts are idle ones, since he has not taken part in any actions.

the rebels i.e. Bonnie Prince Charlie, the young pretender, Cumberland
 eventually putting down the rebellion at Culloden in April 1746.
when the late rebellion was at the highest i.e. as they marched towards
 Derby from where, in December, they were to retreat. The date here is
 towards the end of November 1745.
the Protestant religion i.e. in support of George II.
the gauntlope i.e. the gauntlet, running between two lines and being hit as
 he goes.
halberd This represented the rank of sergeant.

Chapter 12

Retrospect on the lieutenant, with the vagaries of fortune he has
suffered. The officers argue: Northerton reveals himself to be particularly revolting; Jones shows that he is a man of integrity and religion.
Because of this he is picked upon by Northerton but more than holds
his own and injures the other by his sarcasm. The insults to Sophia are
calculated to rouse Tom's anger, and they do. The felling of Tom and
the arrest of Ensign Northerton make a dramatic end to the chapter,
with the landlady the only one showing any presence of mind in her
attempts to revive Tom.

Tannieres Better known as Malplaquet, September 1709, where
 Marlborough defeated the French.
the Duke of Marlborough (1650–1722) The great general much admired
 by Fielding.
nice regard i.e. his being particular about.
the Trojans to the cackling of geese See Pope's *Iliad*, 3,1–13 (for 'geese'
 read 'cranes').
Madam Dacière Madame Dacière translated the *Iliad* and the *Odyssey* in
 1711 and 1716 respectively.
von woman i.e. Helen of Troy.
Homo Northerton's mistake for Homer.
Corderius Cordier (1479–1564) a French Protestant.
put Bumpkin.
nick . . . cull . . . pimp Outwit . . . dupe . . . a corrupt person.
O Monsieur, on ne parle pas . . . la guerre . . . O Sir, one should not
 speak of religion during war.
Smoke the prig i.e. mock, let's mock this priggish youngster.
repartees Clever replies.
hold half a dozen of Burgundy i.e. bet half a dozen bottles of wine.
had both her and her aunt i.e. sexually.
Begar, me no tush de Engliseman . . . By God, I won't touch the dead
 Englishman; I have heard that the English hang the man who touches him
 last.
drawer Server in an inn.

Chapter 13

There is some humour in the landlady's errors, the lieutenant shows his integrity, and the landlady shows herself capable of unsaying all she has said, as well as uttering criticism of being heavily taxed. The complacency, superiority and ignorance of the surgeon are stressed through his comments, another satire on doctors. Notice that the actual suggestions for treatment come from the landlady. Tom reveals his courage by being willing to take on Northerton in his weakened state. He behaves honourably and shows full Christian awareness.

desarts . . . parsons . . . oft . . . thoft Deserts . . . persons . . . ought . . . thought.
window-lights The tax imposed in 1696 on windows. Large dwellings were hard hit, and many boarded-up windows and lived in darkened and unventilated rooms as a result.
resolved him i.e. responded to him.
nemo repente fuit turpissimus Juvenal *Satires*, 2,83 – no man reaches the depths of badness all at once.
divellicated Pulled apart.
sizy i.e. like size, paste.
sack-whey Mixture of weak milk and wine.
take him out i.e. challenge him to a duel.
buss Kiss.

Chapter 14

Even here money rules, and the sergeant's attempt to swindle Tom over the sword demonstrates this. Tom is no fool, but the sergeant is despicable for trying to take advantage of him while he is in a weakened condition. Note the distortion and lies of the sergeant, and the excitement generated by the atmosphere, the time of night, and the prospect of action. There is an element of grotesque humour in the sentinel firing his piece and then falling flat on his face. The ghost, the fears, balance the climax, or anti-climax, of Northerton's disappearance.

bolster Long under-pillow (as today).
battle of Dettingen 15 June 1745, in which George II led his army and defeated the French.
in sensu praedicto In the sense already defined.
so much out of the way i.e. so very expensive.
the bloody Banquo See *Macbeth*, 3,4 and 4,1.
report of the firelock i.e. bang of the gun.
flambeaux Candlesticks or torches.

Chapter 15

The fears of Northerton, with a Fielding digression on the scaffold. The landlady plays a leading part, once more money talks, and exaggeration too comes into it, with the landlady saying that Tom is near death (just as later Tom is to be told that Fitzpatrick will die). Hypocrisy is shown in the landlady's trying to get the sentinel blamed for the escape.

a certain wooden edifice i.e. the scaffold.
quomodo Manner in which the thing was to be accomplished.

Revision questions on Book 7

1 Write an essay on the part played by Mrs Honour in this Book.

2 Is Sophia just a straightforward simple girl? Give reasons from the text for your answer.

3 What do you consider to be the most exciting incident in this book and why?

4 Show how Fielding uses either (a) contemporary events or (b) digressions to enhance the narrative.

5 Write a study of any two of the minor characters who make their appearance in this book.

6 'Money is the root of all evil'. How far do you think Fielding believes this in these chapters?

Book 8

Chapter 1

The opening discusses the marvellous in literature and asserts the view that authors have a responsibility to keep 'within the bounds of possibility'. Fielding deals humorously with Homer. He advises authors to be sparing in their use of ghosts. The historian must record matters as he finds them, within the bounds of probability. He cites classical and a contemporary analogy, and has a knock at contemporary theatre, where evil characters suddenly become good in the last act.

prolegomenous i.e. as a prologue.

M. Dacier The husband of Ann Dacier, he translated Aristotle's *Poetics* in 1692.

Pope . . . Odysseus . . . Phaeacians The reference is to William Broome's comments on the tenth book of the *Odyssey*, where he says that Homer makes the episodes of Circe and Polyphemus 'within the degrees of probability'.

Polypheme *Odyssey*, Book 9.

Circe *Odyssey*, Book 10.

Horace . . . *Ars Poetica*, 191–92.

had an intent . . . his own country The irony is that Fielding does some of this himself.

Hudibras See note p.43.

Hippocrene or Helicon The latter was a mountain in Boeotia, which contained the springs of Hippocrene and Aganippe, the first being the source of poetic inspiration.

mummery Ostentatious, fake ceremony.

Aristotle See *Poetics*, 24,19.

Xerxes ?519–465 BC, the Persian king who led his army against Greece. He achieved an initial success at Thermopylae but his fleet was beaten at Salamis (480). Herodotus was the famous Greek historian who wrote of this war.

Alexander . . . Arrian Arrian told the story of Alexander's campaigns, in seven books.

Agincourt . . . Harry the fifth The defeat of the French in 1415.

Charles the Twelfth . . . Narva He defeated the Russians who were besieging Narva in 1700.

George Villiers The story is told of how Sir George Villiers appeared as a ghost to his son the Duke of Buckingham.

the incredulous hatred mentioned by Horace See *Ars Poetica*, 188.

Trajan . . . Antoninus . . . Nero . . . Caligula The first two, good Roman emperors; the second two, evil and licentious ones.

Fisher . . . Derby Fielding describes the circumstantial details of a case from 10 April 1727, when the attorney Fisher murdered his benefactor Darby in the Inner Temple. He escaped before his trial.

scrutore Desk.

Temple i.e. the Inner Temple, law courts.

Suetonius In *The Lives of the Caesars* 6,34,4.

chaulked Indicated.

-Quis credit . . . Who could credit it? No one, by Hercules! perhaps one or two, perhaps no one.

rarae aves Literally, 'rare birds'; here, unusual people.

a distich a unit of two verse lines, often a couplet.

Tyburn i.e. where the public hangings occurred.

The great art of all poetry . . . The author is Pope.

Chapter 2

The landlady proves to be as cunning as Mrs Honour in her propitiation of Jones. She knows how to bring Sophia into the conversation. It relieves us and Tom from her non-stop monologue of complaints about the behaviour of officers etc. Lies are the order of her day. Her behaviour changes rapidly when she realizes that Tom has very little money.

sparks Wild young men.
narrow . . . arrow Never . . . any.
ordinary A meal provided at a fixed price.
wore a head i.e. of hair.
Angels are painted . . . like her . . . From Thomas Otway's *Venice Preserved* (1682).

Chapter 3

The landlady's sharpness is evident, since she picked up her information about Sophia from the lieutenant. There is irony in the fact that the surgeon discovers that Jones's pulse is disordered (he is thinking about Sophia). Again his use of learned words is parodied, but there is worse to come – the surgeon exemplifies greed too. He learns that Jones has little money, Jones refuses to be blooded and the doctor, against his professional oaths, leaves his patient in a bad way.

animadverting Discussing, criticizing.
a revulsion The withdrawal of inflammation from one part of the body by bleeding another part.
swinging Large.
paymaster i.e. who will pay you.
arrant scrub disreputable fellow.
oft Ought.

Chapter 4

Tom is treated discourteously when he gets up, but the landlady shows her susceptibility to him. Detail on the idiosyncrasies of Benjamin, his Latin tags, his odd humour which appeals to Tom. The latter satisfies his hunger, but we notice that when he appears he is the subject of gossip by the landlady. This gossip is largely confirmed by Benjamin, who is obviously destined to play some role in events.

the Barber of Bagdad In volume 2 of *The Arabian Nights*. He is a boaster.
Don Quixote Cervantes' novel, the barber's name being Nicholas.

a frock a loose gown; a kind of dressing gown.

Festina lente Make haste slowly.

non omnia . . . From Vergil, *Eclogues*, 'We can't all do everything.'

capping verses i.e. providing the endings.

non tanti . . . 'I don't think I am worthy of such honour'.

tondenti gravior 'Troublesome to the one who is shaving'.

hinc illae lachrymae 'Hence proceed all those tears.'

hiatus in manuscriptis i.e. a gap in the manuscript.

Adonis The handsome youth loved by Aphrodite and killed by a wild boar.

statu quo As it was.

lucus a non lucendo The grove is thus called because it denies the shining (From Ovid, *Metamorphoses*).

bye blow Illegitimate offspring.

Chapter 5

Partridge now proceeds (for it is Partridge, the schoolmaster) to ingratiate himself with Tom by referring to the past, though Tom is still suspicious and wishes to be incognito. Yet Partridge shows some insight in pointing out to Tom that his enemies must have discredited him to Allworthy in order to explain that good man's treatment of him. He has found out what he wants to know, but he has not revealed himself to Tom or to the reader.

doctissime tonsorum . . . Most learned of barbers.

Ago tibi . . . I thank you, master.

Proh deum atque . . . By the faith of Gods and men.

ille optimus . . . That best of all patrons.

casu incognito Some unknown misfortune.

Pauca verba Few words.

non si male nunc . . . If we fare badly today it will not always be so.

amoris abundantia . . . An abundance of love towards you.

the rebellion in the North . . . i.e. Bonnie Prince Charlie's landing in Scotland and his subsequent advance into England.

Pro deum atque . . . By the faith of Gods and men.

tempus edax rerum From Ovid, 'Time, devourer of things.'

Erasmi Colloquia . . . All schoolboy texts.

Stowe's Chronicle This ranges up to the year 1580, and is by the celebrated antiquarian John Stow (c. 1525–1605).

Echard's *Roman History* See note p.53. (Also spelt Eachard.)

the *Craftsman* A Tory journal of the time.

Thomas à Kempis (1380–1471) Augustinian monk, author of the *Imitation of Christ* (1441).

Tom Brown's works (1663–1704) A satirist called a 'scribbler' by Fielding.

Chapter 6

The coming together of Tom Jones and the barber is made easier by the fact that Partridge is able to dress his wound. He then reveals who he is – important to the plot since he asserts that he is not Tom's father. He continues eccentric but not greedy; all he wants is to play Sancho Panza to Tom's Don Quixote, though neither man nor their author would see them in quite this way.

at a cut i.e. in attending a wound.
tonsor Barber.
Ars omnibus . . . The art of healing is common to all those who practise it.
I will answer i.e. testify.
infandum, regina . . . This is from the second book of the *Aeneid* 'Beyond all words O Queen is the grief you bid me revive.'
vis unita fortior United strength is the more powerful.
nil desperandum . . . Nothing is to be despaired of under Teuce's rule and Teuce's powers (from Horace).

Chapter 7

Partridge has his own cunning thoughts about persuading Tom to return to his father (as he believes Allworthy to be). Tom shows himself once more to be lacking in caution and to naively accept the situation. There is an ironic account of the indolent landlord and the nature of his marriage. There is a further digression on overcharging.

smart-money See note p. 38

Chapter 8

Based on a factual inn, the author commends the Bell and has one or two snipes at 'the pernicious principles of Methodism'. An important plot point is the introduction of Dowling, the lawyer who brought the news of Mrs Blifil's death to Blifil as Allworthy lay ill. The presence of the 'petty-fogger' leads to more satirical observations, but this man's vicious gossip about Tom is another instance of the prevalence of lying. Tom, offended by the landlady's changed attitude towards him, courts further adventure by leaving.

Whitefield George Whitefield, as influential as Wesley himself in the development of Methodism.
a long hood i.e. covered herself out of modesty and her faith.
Lidlinch It is in Dorset, a few miles from the border of Somerset.

timbersome Reticent, timid.
wished he could divide himself into twenty pieces Compare this with
  the account of him in Book 5 Chapter 7, page 229.

Chapter 9

The chapter opens with a mock-romantic description of nature.
Tom's romantic comparisons are offset by Partridge's down-to-earth
feeling of the cold, and their disagreement as to which direction to
take. Tom is romantically thinking of Sophia, but he is also thinking of
death in the service of his country. Partridge is thinking of food, but
there is an irony in the fact that he is a silent Jacobite while Tom is an
outspoken patriot in the cause of King George. Partridge has heard it
said that Tom was knocked down because he was a Jacobite, hence
the misunderstanding. Partridge cunningly conceals his principles,
being convinced that his future self-interest lies with Tom.

highest order . . . lowest order Note the antithetical balance of this, and
  the mocking of snobbery involved.
Milton, who hath certainly excelled . . . Particularly in *Paradise Lost*.
per devia rura viarum through country byways.
interdum stultus . . . Sometimes a fool speaks at the right moment.
I prae . . . You go first, I will follow you.
Tramontane Coming from the far side of the mountains.
Infandum regina . . . A common quotation of Partridge's.
Prince Charles i.e. the Young Pretender.
the miller with three thumbs . . . A reference to the fact that the Jacobites
  relied on superstitutions for their support, a quality Fielding mocked.
King George i.e. George II (1727–60).
Briareus In Greek mythology, the giant with three hundred hands.
tall long-sided dame . . . Hudibras i.e. fame.
monster of Virgil *Aeneid*, 4,181–3 – fame.
like Ward's pill Joseph Ward (1685–1761) invented a pill that killed as
  many people as it cured.

Chapter 10

Tom is still intent on melancholy, Partridge still frightened of ghosts.
The arrival at the house shows the effect Jones's personality produces
on people, and the abject state of Partridge's imagination as he
considers the old woman a witch. The house itself reflects the man,
and the old woman's description, while it scares Partridge, forecasts
for the reader the state and nature of The Man of the Hill. Tom is able
to indulge his curiosity when he saves the man from the robbers.
Obviously the old man feels some sympathetic rapport between
himself and Tom.

Otway . . . Orphan *The Orphan* or *The Unhappy Marriage* (1680) contains a description of a 'wrinkled hag'.

James 1st (1603–25) He wrote a tract against witches. The laws against them were not repealed until 1746.

virtuoso Skilled in arts and antiquities.

parity i.e. comparability.

Chapter 11

Clear, straightforward narrative, concentrating on the main incidents, but this tale is holding up the progress of the main narrative. It is a study in corruption with a strong moral tone. Debauchery is followed by theft and flight, and Tom's betrayal by his mistress who has been the mistress of many others. Humour is provided by Partridge's unpredictable interruptions. One of these leads to his telling his own story of the ghost that turns out to be a calf with a white face. Fielding is contrasting the gullibility of Partridge in these matters with the gullibility of the man of the hill, which led to his degradation.

Xantippe See note p.32. She was shrewish.

under-part i.e. a subsidiary role.

escritoire Desk.

chaise Carriage.

the great Cirencester road It connected Gloucester with London.

habeas corpus You may have the body, i.e. a person must be brought before a court.

Hindon A village in Wiltshire.

Justice Willoughby of Noyle A friend of Fielding's and a principal witness in the Darby murder case.

recognizance i.e. surety.

Lord Justice Page Popularly – and unpopularly – known as the hanging judge.

Chapter 12

The old man describes his poverty in London, then his meeting with Watson, who praises him for having committed the robbery in Oxford. This shows the depths of the society in which he is mixing. Imagery of medicine and business accompanies the degrading introduction to gambling. This chapter is a study in plundering and swindling.

Leadenhall A large London provisions market.

irritamenta malorum . . . The incitement to evil, riches are obtained by digging.

the Friars i.e. Blackfriars, situated in London between the Thames and
Ludgate Hill.
abashment i.e. shame.
little doctors . . . Note the image.
queer cull Worthless dupe.
the board was sitting i.e. the gamblers were ready.
run a levant to place a bet but clear off if you lose.
rum cull i.e. one who might be awkward.
score it behind the door Equivalent to today's 'put it on the slate'.
make a bold brush Leave hurriedly.

Chapter 13

This examines the ups and downs of the gambler's life, the moral
emphasis on such degradation still apparent. We are invited to
suspend our disbelief when the man meets his father by chance and
then mends his ways. There is no preparation for his sudden conver-
sion, but his sermon to his listeners is a telling exposition of Christian
behaviour as well as an expression of devotion to the classical
philosophers. He comes to the conclusion that the great philosophers
make for temporal happiness, whereas faith makes for an eternal
happiness'.

sharpers Card sharpers, swindlers.
of the calling i.e. gambling.
the Serjeant-Surgeon An anachronism, since the man of the hill is
referring to a period before the Monmouth rebellion of 1685, while
Fielding's friend 'R' is John Ranby, who had been appointed
Serjeant-Surgeon to George II in 1740.
tempus edax rerum 'O Time, devourer of things'.
Fortis . . . See translation in footnote, p.422.) A paraphrase by Fielding of
Juvenal's *Satires*, 2,7,86–8.

Chapter 14

The debate between the Man of the Hill and Watson. The former
proves himself compassionate but naive in giving Watson the money,
since he gambles with it immediately. The news of Monmouth's
landing is a deliberate parallel, in Fielding's structure, with the
contemporary rebellion of 1745. The irony is that the apothecary's
news is false. There follows a detailed history of the politics of the
time, obviously with the contemporary parallel in mind. Tom in fact
refers to this, to the surprise of the reclusive old man, who reveals his
betrayal by Watson – that compares with other betrayals in the novel.

set up Begin again.

broken merchant i.e. failed and bankrupt gambler.

the Duke of Monmouth (1649–85) Illegitimate son of Charles II, attempted to seize the throne from the Catholic Duke of York in 1685. His forces were defeated at Sedgemore, and he was beheaded, his followers being mercilessly slaughtered on the orders of the King.

advices i.e. items of news.

humour i.e. trait.

King James James II (1685–88), a Roman Catholic.

against a king i.e. George II.

varium & mutabile semper Virgil says that a woman is always varying and changeable.

joined the Duke at Bridgewater i.e. the Duke of Monmouth.

Cullumpton In Devon, twelve miles from Exeter. (Now spelt Cullompton.)

Wellington Six miles from Taunton in Somerset.

the news of the Glorious Revolution i.e. the accession of the Protestant William of Orange and Mary in 1688 and the deposition of James II.

Chapter 15

The real subject of this chapter is the similarity of human nature regardless of race, plus the religious attitude of the man of the hill. Tom reveals his own optimism in the face of the pessimistic appraisal of human nature the man presents.

valets à louage Menservants for hire.

a knave is dressed like a fop i.e. a criminal looks like a man of fashion.

wanted employment Lacked occupation.

palling i.e. those which pall, become boring.

stews Brothels.

jakes Urinals.

day and night . . . seasons to him As, indeed, were they to Milton in his blindness – and the man of the hill is blind to the goodness of human nature.

Revision questions on Book 8

1 Indicate the part played by Partridge in this Book.

2 Consider Tom's experiences in inns with landlords and landladies. What do they tell you of the life of the time?

3 What do you consider to be important in the man of the hill's narrative?

4 What do you consider to be the main moral points that are made in this Book?

5 In what ways is this Book important to the working out of the plot? Give reasons for your answer.

Book 9

Chapter 1

Fielding writes here against imitators of his method in *Tom Jones*. He says that for the kind of history he is writing genius is essential. It involves invention and judgement plus 'a good share of learning', and learning of one's own times. He considers that conversation is important too, and that this must be taken from life. The writer must know 'all ranks and degrees of men'. He must also have 'a good heart, and be capable of feeling'.

two or three authors . . . Probably Fielding's rivals, Richardson and Smollett.

braying in the lion's skin The ass who disguised himself thus but was recognized by his voice and ears in *Aesop's Fables*.

Rowe Nicholas Rowe (1674–1718), editor of Shakespeare and author of a tragedy *Jane Shore* in imitation of Shakespeare.

the Romans were of Cato Horace, *Epistles*, 1,19.

***Scribimus* . . .** See foot of page 436 in Penguin.

numbers i.e. metric feet, regularity, poetry.

pruritus A bodily itch, here an itch to write.

genius Horace's *Ars Poetica*, 409–10.

belles lettres (Fr.) Literary works.

the ornament of numbers i.e. were excellent poets.

Mr Miller Philip Miller (1691–1771) FRS, author of *The Gardeners Dictionary* in 2 vols, 1731 and 1739.

Johnson, Wycherly Samuel Johnson (1709–84) the greatest man of letters of the 18th century and compiler of the first important dictionary of the English Language, and William Wycherley (c.1640–1716), author of the Restoration Comedy *The Country Wife*.

a Cibber or a Clive Susan Cibber was married to Colley Cibber's son. She was admired as a singer by Handel and she was a distinguished tragic actress. Catherine Clive was a fine comedy actress.

e converso On the contrary.

The author who will make me weep, says Horace *Ars Poetica* 102–3.

Chapter 2

The fine view moves Tom to romantic thoughts of Sophia, but when they enter the wood we have a graphic incident described. Sexual attraction between Jones and the rescued lady is immediate, and the coincidence that the man is Northerton is just about acceptable in the area. We remark the coolness of the Man of the Hill through all this. Northerton's escape is predictable, the lady's flirtation with Tom in view of his undeniable physical attraction understandable too.

AURORA Goddess of dawn.
Mazard Hill Fictitious, but perhaps the Worcestershire Beacon, highest of the Malvern Hills and with a splendid view.
parole i.e. word of honour.
Orpheus and Eurydice Ovid, *Metamorphoses*, 10,1–6. Orpheus was allowed to redeem his dead wife from Hades by leading her out behind him, having promised never to look back. He broke his word, and lost her for ever.

Chapter 3

The character of the inn of good reputation is spelt out ironically, and of course the lady's appearance goes against her and Tom. The latter innocently makes things worse by asking for clothes for the lady. There is a fight, which is done in Fielding's most zestful manner, and there is the usual coincidence of the unexpected, namely the arrival of Partridge, followed by the entrance of the lady and then Susan the Chambermaid.

temple of Vesta The Roman Goddess of the heart and of fire; vestal virgins were always in attendance at the temple.
concubinage i.e. mistresses and prostitutes.
Desdemona . . . Cassio Othello, Act 3, Scene 3 and Act 4, Scene 1.
the unfortunate Moor i.e. Othello.
two-handed i.e. strong in both arms.
Thalestris She was the Queen of the Amazons who travelled with her women to meet Alexander with the aim of producing a race of great strength.
Victory . . . Fortune The personifications emphasize the mock-epic tone.
the poor unfortunate Helen i.e. the lady rescued by Tom, compared here to Helen of Troy.

Chapter 4

With the arrival of the soldiers the lady is revealed as Mrs Waters, and the landlady makes her abject apologies – in the cause of her own self-interest. Mrs Waters at first reveals her intolerance and snobbery, but Tom as usual acts as peacemaker, and dispenses forgiveness all round. He is followed by Partridge, diplomatic international language conveying their 'league'. There is some kindly irony about the inevitable drinking bout that follows.

his billets i.e. rooms for his men.
pillowbere Pillowcase.
libation A toast, strictly to the gods, in Greek mythology.

Chapter 5

A short digression (for Fielding) on the nature of heroes, but with the war, so to speak, over, Tom is able to give some attention to Mrs Waters, who is certainly giving her attention to him. There is a detailed description of Tom's attractions. Mrs Waters employs 'the whole artillery of love' upon him, and again the mock-heroic mode of analogy is used by Fielding. It is done with a kind of grotesque humour that makes Tom's surrender almost acceptable.

Ulysses The remark is appropriate; *Tom Jones* is an eating novel, as the film made very clear!
Hercules Greek hero noted for his immense strength in performing twelve labours.
Adonis See note p.67.
Cremona fiddle This is the town in Lombardy where the violin of Stradivari (1644–1737) was made.
Pasiphae See Ovid, *Metamorphoses*. Pasiphae disguises herself in a wooden cow she has had made, because she is attracted to a bull.
spicula & faces amoris The stings and flames of love.
beaus Fashionable men about town.
preserved his votary i.e. took care of his worshipper.
dignus vindice nodus . . . Let not a god interfere, unless there is a worthy knot to untangle.
every engine of amorous warfare Note the image, for she is now using the whole battery or artillery on Tom.
a kind of Dutch defence The press at the time was full of stories of unnecessary Dutch surrenders to the French.

Chapter 6

This is a necessary filling-in of the background of Mrs Waters. The serjeant gives the account, but is interrupted by Partridge, who provides a distorted account of himself and Tom which excites the landlady. There is the usual below-stairs argument, which ends in a fight between coachman and serjeant, but the reader is perhaps more interested in the fact that the young lady is delayed from leaving because of the coachman's injuries.

loves the cloth i.e. respects religion.
Veritas odium parit Truth begets hatred (Terence, *Andria*).
numscull's pate The head of an idiot.
rip up i.e. dig up, bring to attention.
Sed hei mihi . . . Alas! I am not what I was.
denimated Titled.
Amici sumus We are friends.
swinging See note p.66.
humours See note p.27.
Harkeet Listen.
nonsequitur A statement with little or no relevance to what has preceded it.
an If.
She could feast heartily at the table of love . . . The eating image is here equated with sexual appetite.

Chapter 7

Fielding is deliberately ironic, even coy, about Mrs Waters's relationship with Northerton, though the fact that she agrees to accompany him is itself damning. Again greed rules in Northerton's assault on her, but Fielding is careful at the end of the chapter to make it clear that no reflection on the army in general is intended.

till the end . . . campaign . . . rebels Note how Fielding keeps up a running commentary on the major events at the back of the personal incidents.

Revision questions on Book 9

1 What kind of a woman do you think Mrs Waters is? Give reasons for your answer.

2 Estimate the part played by fights in this Book.

3 What do you consider to be the funniest episode in this book? You should refer closely to the text to support your views.

Book 10

Chapter 1

Fielding warns the reader as critic not to rush into judgement or to condemn any parts of this work until he has studied the whole, and to distinguish between individual characters who appear to have much in common. He asks for compassion and tolerance rather than condemnation.

no wiser than some of his editors . . . Fielding had already satirized two of these, Theobald and Warburton.

Sir Epicure Mammon, and Sir Fopling Flutter . . . Sir Courtly Nice
The first the caricature in Jonson's *The Alchemist* (1610), the second in Etherege's *The Man of Mode* (1676) and the third in a play by John Crowne in 1685.

Dido The tragic character in Virgil's *Aeneid*.

nulla virtute . . . Juvenal, *Satires* 4,2–3 translation at foot of page in Penguin (468).

quas humana . . . Horace *Ars Poetica* – see note on Book 11 Chapter 1 for the complete quotation.

Chapter 2

Wonderful mock-heroic opening to the chapter by contrasting man and nature at night, followed by the graphic description of the gentleman's arrival, and the incidents that ensue as a result of mistaken identity. There is considerable excitement, almost of a farcical nature, as battle is once more joined. Note Mrs Fitzpatrick's presence of mind, and Tom's ability also to adapt to the situation. Fielding's irony plays amusedly over this deception.

some modern connoisseurs in music Note the sarcasm, obviously directed at some contemporary singers.

posture State.

post i.e. post haste.

Mrs Behn's novels Aphra Behn (1640–89) novelist and dramatist, some of her works being of questionable taste – hence Fielding's sarcasm here.

bate Greatly annoyed.

was never blown upon before i.e. never criticised.

breach of privilege Again, a light-hearted piece of sarcasm.

Chapter 3

Susan deceives her mistress over the bribe from Fitzpatrick but ironically the landlady does not believe the truth about Tom and Mrs Waters. She herself has swindled them anyway. She also reveals her greed, and we learn that Mr Fitzpatrick has already spent his wife's fortune. The comings and goings of the night provide plenty of narrative tension. With the arrival of the beautiful lady and her maid this is increased, for we suspect from their behaviour who they are.

Worcestershire perry i.e. wine made from pears.
errant scrubs Disreputable characters.
mulled Wine heated with sugar and spices to make a hot drink.

Chapter 4

The ill-breeding of the waiting-woman who has just arrived is described. Her greed and her nicety and arrogance are all defined, and she shows her ignorance in her snobbery and her not understanding Partridge. But she is amazed by the news that Tom is in the house, and once more a chapter ends on a note of expectation.

to regale . . . dainties Treat herself to the food.
fourberie Trick.
good quality i.e. gentlefolk.
Abigail Term for a lady's servant (1 Samuel, 25).
Non semper . . . A quotation from a grammar book – it is not always the word with a grammatical case that is the nominative to the verb.
Quare non Why not?

Chapter 5

The maid is of course Mrs Honour, and there is mounting excitement as she hurries to tell Sophia the news. Meanwhile Mrs Honour is abused by the landlady, and Partridge is unwise enough to include Sophia in his denunciations. He is silly enough to then tell Mrs Honour when she reappears that Tom is 'in bed with a wench'. This causes Honour to exaggerate to Sophia in turn, but Susan the chambermaid, urged on by Honour, gives the whole game away, and thus injures Sophia's feelings. They are further hurt by Partridge's gossip about her being repeated. The leaving of her muff is the symbolic rejection of Tom.

As in the month of June . . . Fielding in mock-romantic strain.

'Never a barrel the better herring' i.e. there is nothing to choose between them.

Noscitur a socio He is known by his company.

Bath trulls i.e. prostitutes.

non omnia . . . All things are not in the power of all.

Jackanapes Impertinent conceited person.

ripped up i.e. deliberately reintroduced.

easy Comforted (the reverse of the truth).

Chapter 6

Partridge shows that he is alive to the opportunity of taking advantage by stealing the horses at the inn. Tom reprimands him, then sees the message left by Sophia. His is a natural distraction, but we are also kept informed of the likely pursuit of the ladies by Mr Fitzpatrick, in the belief that he is following his wife.

repeated only the word king i.e. so that he does not give away the fact that he supports the young pretender's cause.

horrida bella Fearsome wars.

the information annexed The message attached to it.

Mr King of Bath Probably Thomas King, who ran a coach service between London, Bath and Bristol.

Chapter 7

Mr Western's arrival, together with the emphasis on chance, which means that he misses Sophia and Mrs Fitzpatrick, who is his niece. Western further confuses everybody by his use of jargon, and the appearance of the muff contributes to the excitement and the uncertainty and the recriminations. The ridiculous charge against Jones for stealing the muff is explored, and the departure of everyone in pursuit of those they follow maintains the narrative flow of excitement.

a stolen match i.e. an elopement.

Bedlam The madhouse (after the hospital of St Mary of Bethlehem in London).

commission of the peace i.e. a magistrate.

coadjutor i.e. fellow judge.

commitment i.e. an order for him to be detained.

Chapter 8

Retrospect on the escape of Sophia in order to bring the reader up to date. The quarrel between Western and his sister is entirely predictable, and calculated to provoke the one and the other because of the way they apportion blame. Blifil proves to be his usual sycophantic self.

E'en such a man . . . Henry IV, Part 2, Act 1, Scene 1, line 70.
Hercules that of Hylas The latter was drowned while hunting, and Hercules continued to call his name while searching for him.
Ovid hath belied her sex Metapmorphoses 3 (Echo was the nymph in love with Narcissus).
Salique Law The law which laid down that males of the male line only could succeed to the throne, women being thus excluded.

Chapter 9

Retrospect continues, with the means of Sophia's escape. Sophia shows good sense, even cunning, in the way she chooses to go, but Fielding indulges his humour by a commonplace explanation of the horse's stopping on Sophia's account. Honour persuades Sophia to change her direction, but her own vacillations mean that she still continues to move on against Honour's advice. This chopping and changing indicates the state of Sophia's mind.

Arria The wife of Caecina Paetus, who was condemned to die by committing suicide. She set him an example: stabbing herself and then telling him that it did not hurt.
habiliments Garments.
ever that of Anacreon . . . bee-hive Fielding's error, which he later corrected, for it was Plato who had honey deposited on his lips by bees.
like Hudibras *Hudibras*, 1,1,447.
makes the old mare trot The proverbial phrase is 'Money makes the old mare trot.'
certain pecuniary civilities i.e. he hadn't given her any tips, gifts of money.
meat for his master i.e. worthy of someone better than he is.

Revision questions on Book 10

1 Write an analysis of Chapter 1 of this Book, bringing out clearly the main points in Fielding's argument.

2 Indicate the part played by Mrs Waters, Mrs Honour and Mr Fitzpatrick in this Book.

3 Give a clear account of how Sophia escaped from her father's house.

4 Compare and contrast the conduct of Tom and Sophia in Book 10.

Book 11

Chapter 1

Fielding returns to the critics, and condemns them roundly for their condemnations. He is particularly hard on those guilty of slander. He cites Shakespeare in support of his statement. He deplores generalizations while admitting, with Horace, that one line can be dead yet asserting that this should not damn the whole work. Then, tongue in cheek, he emphasizes how cruel it would be if his history were to be condemned because of particular chapters.

Who steals my gold steals trash . . . *Othello*, 3,3,157.
Alas Thou hast written no book Macduff's actual words are 'He has no children' (Act 4, Scene 3) in speaking of Macbeth in the tragedy of that name.
Longinus 2nd century AD, supposed author of the famous Greek work of literary criticism, *On The Sublime*.
Bossu René Le Bossu (1631–80) French critic.
foro literario In the literary court.
Verum ubi plura . . . *Ars Poetica* 351–3.
Martial . . . *Epigrams* 1,16.
hazard Place at risk.

Chapter 2

Tension as Sophia knows herself to be pursued, and in doing a good turn to the other lady she is thrown from her horse. With daylight comes the recognition (strange this, since one would have thought that they would recognize each other's voice), but Fielding is teasing the reader somewhat here. The arrival at yet another inn is described, with the grotesque incident of another tumble for Sophia and the coarseness of the bystanders. The landlord, quite a character, now speculates and comes to the conclusion that Sophia is Jenny Cameron.

the young Chevalier . . . the Duke's army i.e. the young Pretender and the British Commander, the Duke of Cumberland.

news arrived . . . honest Frenchmen Rumours current at the time (reported in the *True Patriot* 10 December 1745) proved to be unfounded.

Madam Jenny Cameron (1699(?)–1767), supposed to be the mistress of the young Pretender, but the stories about her were exaggerated. She was about forty-six at the time.

Chapter 3

Comparison between Sophia and Mrs Fitzpatrick, with the latter eclipsed by Sophia's beauty. They stay at the inn; Sophia is well treated by the landlady because of who she thinks Sophia is.

Chapter 4

Another retrospective narration which fills in the details of Mrs Fitzpatrick's life. It may be compared with the Man of the Hill's story in terms of what it reveals of human nature. Corruption, opportunism, the power of gossip and deception, all are evident. The nature of Mr Fitzpatrick is fully exposed, and the weakness of Mrs Fitzpatrick just as directly indicated.

dégagé Easy, detached in manner.

rusticated i.e. having the manners of the country.

Scandal Club i.e. the gossip-mongers.

his designs . . . To rob a lady of her fortune by way of marriage. This is the way of the world in *Tom Jones* and in much of 18th-century society.

from the Pump The Pump Room, where one received the beneficial waters.

leading-strings Used to keep control of a young child.

Mr Nash The celebrated Beau Nash (1674–1761), the gambler and Master of Ceremonies at Bath in 1704.

Bedlam See note p.79.

Chapter 5

Mr Fitzpatrick's deception discovered, his being intent on marrying either niece or aunt for their money, and his continuing lies to Mrs Fitzpatrick are probed. Mrs Fitzpatrick shows her own capacity for self-deception. The lifestyle with her husband is a degrading one.

the Rooms The Assembly Rooms either for dancing or for playing cards.

draw on you . . . at fourteen days i.e. insist on your paying up.

Chamont mentions in the *Orphan* See note p.70 to Otway's play where Chamont meets the witch.

Book 12

Chapter 1

Fielding defends his method of including in his own works extracts from learned authors. He excuses himself from the accusation of plagiarism, and refers to the ancient authors as 'a rich common, where every person who hath the smallest tenement in Parnassus hath a free right to fatten his muse'. He gives an example of genuine plagiarism.

Abbé Bannier (1673–1741) Whose mythology was translated into English, 1739–41.
Parnassus The home of the Muses in Greek mythology.
robbing the spittal Robbing the hospital – stealing, making a profit in a despicable manner.
one Mr Moore (1702–1734) His play *The Rival Modes* was produced in 1727. It contained lines by Pope, which the latter wanted taken out. Pope had his revenge by including Moore in his satirical poem *The Dunciad*.

Chapter 2

Western, who is thoroughly selfish, bemoans the fact that his pursuit of Sophia is costing him good hunting time. By luck he finds a fellow squire out hunting. This leads to his usual self-indulgence of heavy drinking, his return home being the natural aftermath of this.

cross-way Crossroads.
fatigated i.e. fatigued (note the high-flown word used by Supple).
compos voti Granted your wish.
fair Grimalkin . . . Venus The story is told by Sir Roger L'Estrange (1616–1704) in his *Fables of Aesop and Other Eminent Mythologists*.
whistled drunk In a deep state of intoxication.

Chapter 3

Tom has left the inn with Partridge to follow Sophia, and receives from him the same advice as that given to Western, that is, to return home. The fact that he hasn't a home to go to makes him mad temporarily, and his reaction when he recovers is to enlist. Partridge shows his superstition over the Man of the Hill, and he and Tom discuss death, Partridge becoming increasingly hysterical at the prospect of it.

tract Track.

sed vox ea sola . . . But that is the only word I can discover for it.

infandum, regina jubes . . . Beyond all words, O queen . . . (see note
 p.69).

Dulce & decorum est . . . It is sweet and fitting to die for one's country.
 Fielding translates loosely on p.560. *Horace*, Odes 3, 2,13–16.

mors omnibus communis Death is common to all.

non immunes ab illis . . . We are not free from these evils.

Vir bonus est quis? . . . Who is the good man? He who maintains the laws
 of the Fathers and the decrees and ordinances.

Chapter 4

Tom reprimands Partridge for having so little charity when they meet
the beggar. The discovery of the book and the bank-bill leads to
Tom's being in a rapture about Sophia. He rewards the beggar, who
displays that common ingredient of human nature, greed, and tries to
get more money.

toyman i.e. a salesman and jeweller, seller of trinkets.

action of trover i.e. an action bought to recover goods from a person to
 whom they do not belong.

orandum est ut . . . We must pray for a sound mind in a sound body
 (Juvenal, *Satire*, 10).

ben't Is not to be.

Chapter 5

The noise of the drum arouses expectation, Partridge virtually
confirms his cowardice by his reactions, and thinks he sees ghosts
when in reality he hears the noises of a puppet-show. Tom wants the
simplicity of Punch and Joan, but the puppet-master shows that even
in his profession there are degrees of snobbery.

mens sana in corpore sano A sound mind in a sound body.

the crown and coffin The Pretender's flag seen at a distance might appear
 like this – in fact Charles had promised his father that he would give him
 the three crowns of Great Britain or himself dead in his coffin.

beats up i.e. tries to attract customers.

a prompter i.e. keeping to the image, an appetizer.

the *Provok'd Husband* By Colley Cibber, produced in 1628. Fielding
 thought it dull.

highly in nature True to life.

dancer of wires The puppet-master.

Chapter 6

What is enacted on stage in the puppetry is now extended to life with the maid and the Merry-Andrew, thus disproving the heavy harangue of the puppet-master on the good morality of his shows. The usual inn scene follows the row, with Tom sleeping (with the muff) and the rest round the fire, drinking.

Merry – Andrew The clown.
Jephtha's Rash Vow See Judges 11–12.

Chapter 7

Digression on the position of servants with masters – Partridge is boasting about Tom – but Partridge also feels that Tom is somewhat mad. The company readily agrees with him (the implication is that company like this tend to agree with each other). But there is disagreement about the treatment that should be applied to Tom. At the back of this there continues to be news about the progress of the rebels. This leads to a conversation in which the prejudices and ignorance of each person is revealed in a humorous way.

felix quem faciunt . . . Happy is the man who learns, from the dangers of others, to be cautious.
father dies seized of a right The son should inherit that right when his father dies.
Papishes i.e. Papists.
bumpers Large, brimming glasses.

Chapter 8

Tom, rescuing the Merry-Andrew from the puppet-master, learns that the latter has tried to rob Sophia. Tom shows his inherent goodness by reconciling master and man. When they are caught in the storm and shelter in an alehouse, coincidence further helps them in the person of the boy who rode before Sophia. Fielding defends Tom's sensitivity on Sophia's account by emphasizing that 'I am not writing a system, but a history'.

some choler Anger, temper.
the turn this bout i.e. let's have more to drink – we have something to celebrate.

Chapter 9

The boy is easily bribed, and Jones and Partridge and he follow in the track of Sophia, but they meet – again the arm of coincidence is a long one – the lawyer Dowling. This is an important plot indication of the latter's importance, and our interest is aroused by Tom and Dowling adjourning to a room.

half a crown i.e. 12½p – but worth much more then.
a conceit i.e. an idea.
generally a serjeant i.e. not of high intellect – an ironic aside by Fielding.

Chapter 10

Dowling provokes Tom on the subject of Blifil, and Tom gives a character summary of Blifil based on his experience of him. Dowling affects to be – or is – greatly interested to hear how Tom is thought to be related to Allworthy. Tom reveals his rightness of principle in not coveting Mr Allworthy's fortune, and Dowling reveals that he has a heart by approving of Tom's sentiments.

I have a borough for him . . . i.e. I have got my eye on a borough for which he can stand, for Parliament.
a long train of wicked artifice A succession of cunning schemes.
even from his boyish years . . . *Othello*, 1,3.
Pone me pigris . . . Horace, *Odes* 1,22, lines 17–24.
if we should happen to meet Mr Dowling . . . Note the deliberate vagueness of this so as to keep the reader guessing.

Chapter 11

The boy proves unreliable, in the sense that Jones and Partridge soon get lost. Partridge is convinced that a witch has set them on the wrong course, and a fall from his horse strengthens his opinion. When the boy falls off his horse too Partridge considers this the final proof.

a small matter i.e. some money.

Chapter 12

Partridge is horrified as they approach noise and light. The gypsies give them a welcome, and Fielding gives the reader a digression on the fact that this is not satanic, all the paraphernalia of the infernal regions having been taken over by the managers of playhouses. All the courtesy lacking in society, he says, is shown here by the gypsies, who contrast their way of life with that of more sophisticated society and its governments. The incident with Partridge reflects the rigid standard of justice imposed by the gypsies. The Gypsy King defines the difference between gypsies and society 'My people rob your people and your people rob one another.' There follows a digression on the difficulties of absolute monarchy and the corruption that power exerts.

Beelzebub Any devil or demon, but generally associated with Satan.
Aeneas ... Dum stupet ... While he is standing staring in amazement.
discourse i.e. address.
de parties detache i.e. travelling about.
oder Other.
volution Revolution.
dough Though.
sham Shame.
tieves Thieves.

Chapter 13

Tom's route is traced, so that expectation is aroused because he is getting so near, but not near enough, to Sophia. Again they stop at an inn, and here Partridge shows that he can be devious as he tries to get Tom to use Sophia's money to pay for what they need. Tom is of course outraged by the idea, but as usual the row between them is made up.

deviation i.e. diversion.
Longinus See note p.81. Fielding is here concentrating on narrative directness.
dainty i.e. a present.
fortuna perpetuo est bona Fortune, you are never constant in your kindness (from *Terence*).
non longe alienum ... Not alien to the concerns of Scaevola.
communis ... Common, strange, free serve different cases (an example from a Latin grammar).
in foro conscientiae According to the law of the conscience.
fas & nefas Right and wrong.
nemo omnibus ... No one is always wise.
the vices of a warm disposition i.e. he got over things quickly, he easily forgave and forgot.

Chapter 14

Tom's good nature and gullibility are shown by his letting the stranger accompany them. The incident finds Partridge in the grotesque situation of having been thrown from his horse. Jones's compassion is aroused by the man (another plot link, as we shall discover).

Revision questions on Book 12

1 Write an account of any two adventures in this Book.

2 Compare and contrast the characters of Tom and Partridge as they are revealed by certain incidents.

3 What are the main aspects of human nature revealed in this Book? You should refer to the text in your answer.

4 Give an account of the experience with the gypsies, bringing out fully the moral implications of it.

Book 13

Chapter 1

The author's invocation to fame, with many references to classical analogies and to his own wife, as well as contemporary and grotesque references. He then goes on to instance the importance of Genius and Humanity, Learning and Experience, in his conception of his work.

Mnesis Mnemosyne, the mother of the Muses.
Maeonia Reputedly the place where Homer was born.
Mantua The birthplace of Virgil.
the fair hill Ludgate Hill in London.
in my Charlotte Fielding's first wife who died in 1744.
much plumper Dame The goddess of material gain, profit.
trachtchugt (Du.) Canal boat.
Ufrow Gelt (Ufrow is corruption of Dutch word for Mrs) Mrs Money.
in Grub-street school A London street; the 'home' of hack-writers.
into numbers i.e. serial publication.
Aristophanes . . . A list of writers whom Fielding admired. They are too well-known to need individual comment here with the exception of Pierre Marivaux (1688–1763) the comic/romantic writer, whose novel *La Vie de Marianne*, which began coming out in 1731, influenced Richardson, Fielding's great contemporary.

Allen and Lyttleton Two of Fielding's great friends.
at thy birchen altar A reference to the practice of flogging at Eton.
Warburton (1698–1779) Editor of Shakespeare, known for his erudition,
  was also Bishop of Gloucester.
levee Reception.
spunging-house i.e. where debtors were held.
drum See note p.84.

Chapter 2

Brief digression on fame in posterity at the beginning is followed by
the complications, when Tom and Partridge arrive in London, of their
finding the house where Sophia is. Tom's encounter with the porter
occasions another digression, then a further disappointment because
Tom is at Mrs Fitzpatrick's, but again we are made aware of the
impact he has on women. Mrs Fitzpatrick – mistaken identity again –
believes that he is Blifil, though she soon changes her mind under the
influence of her maid's views.

as Sydenham expresses it (1624–89) An expert on gout.
terrestial Elysian fields In Greek mythology, Elysium was the
  dwelling-place of the blessed after death.
Cerberus Three-headed dog, who guards the entrance to Hades, drugged
  so that Aeneas could pass him.
a sop a drug in the *Aeneid*, here a bribe.
piquet Card game for two people playing with a reduced pack.

Chapter 3

The scheming ideas of Mrs Fitzpatrick are set forth. She goes to Lady
Bellaston with the idea of making all known to Western, thus
double-crossing Sophia. But Lady Bellaston is intrigued by the
description of Tom and, her lust already stirred, arranges to call at
Mrs Fitzpatrick's where she will see him.

intelligence News, information.

Chapter 4

Tom produces the pocket-book. The interruption, and the arrival first
of Lady Bellaston and then the peer, leads to a digression on the
rudeness of polite society. But the plot is furthered, for Lady Bellaston
observes Tom, and although she says that Sophia has nothing to fear
from him, we sense that Tom may have something to fear from Lady
Bellaston.

Non acuta . . . Horace, *Odes*, 1,16,7–8.
pushing in her hoop sideways . . . The whalebone expanded the skirt,
  and made entry into a room difficult.
the relation i.e. the story.

Chapter 5

Jealousy already, as the peer refuses Mrs Fitzpatrick permission to see
Tom. A digression on men of manners as Tom gets an apartment in
the house of a lady who has been helped by Allworthy. He rescues a
young gentleman who is being assaulted by his footman (rescue is one
of Tom's functions in life), and Nightingale, together with Mrs Miller
and her family, now enter the plot.

a scrub A young man of no account.
parts Intelligence, wit.
Vertu Love of fine arts, being a connoisseur.
Will's or Button's Famous London coffee-houses, the first patronized
  earlier by Dryden and the second by Addison.
whisk The game of whist.
my Hoyle Edmond Hoyle (1672–1769) an authority on whist.
history doth not, like a newspaper . . . An ironic glance at the ephemeral
  nature of the press.

Chapter 6

The debate on love reveals the states of mind of Tom and Miss Nancy,
then comes the oblique (some would say direct) invitation to the
masquerade. This gives food for speculation. Nightingale appears to
feel for Nancy what Jones feels for Sophia, though their later fortunes
may be contrasted. Tom himself is suffering financial embarrassment,
a topic that furnishes Fielding with a digression. Despite Partridge's
pressures, Tom will not succumb to using Sophia's money.

Chancellor . . . Archbishop . . . Prime Minister i.e. each at the
  beginning of his career.
a masquerade These entertainments had become quite scandalous, and
  are a target for Fielding's moral comments.
Lombard Street i.e. bankers (in London).
White's Chocolate House A private London club, largely used by
  professional gamblers.

Chapter 7

Opens ironically with the reference to Heydegger, and continues in that vein with the innuendoes of the masquerade. There is a certain fun in the questions of identity, but Tom naively reveals his love for Sophia, supposedly to Mrs Fitzpatrick. The lady appears to be a kind of avenging demon, but Tom finds himself involved with Lady Bellaston. This shows two things: (a) the power of the lady and her determination to have Tom and (b) the importance (to the plot) of Tom's involvement with Lady Bellaston.

Heydegger 'Count' Heidegger (1659–1749), who was very dissolute and organized the society masquerades of the period. He was Swiss.
arbiter deliciarum Judge of delights.
votaries Worshippers.
beat about . . . game i.e. a hunting image.
grand huzza i.e. a loud cheer.
Opera House In London's Haymarket Theatre, where Heidegger was manager.

Chapter 8

Tom is already a kept man, as the bank-note proves. But if the lady's generosity is apparent, Tom's is soon called into action by the story Mrs Miller tells of her cousin. Tom immediately gives her money to relieve their distress, but Nightingale believes they are to blame for their own debts; an interesting moral contrast here.

a quinzy Inflammation of the tonsils, often accompanied by abscesses.
cawdle A warm gruel mixture used to keep up the strength of the sick.
sold by an execution i.e. an order for immediate sale.

Chapter 9

Jones continues to be at the whim of Lady Bellaston and is sorely put out at not finding Sophia, and by thoughts of her particular sufferings. He is also caught up in a kind of gratitude to Lady Bellaston, to whom he owes his present prosperity. The latter is unreliable, as her continual letters to Tom reveal. Expectation is aroused by Lady Bellaston's arranging an assignation with Tom at the house where Sophia is staying, though she has arranged that the latter is safely away at the play.

Like that of the Papists . . . set forth in certain French novels Fielding is drawing an analogy between religious pictures and lewd or erotic pictures of love-making.

Chapter 10

Mrs Miller's cousin turns out to be the robber. There is some pathos in this chapter, but the expressions of gratitude dominate the exchanges.

transporting Uplifting.

Chapter 11

The narrative temperature rises with the unexpected meeting of Tom and Sophia, though it has been hinted at in Chapter 9. The exchanges of the lovers are moving and natural, with the remembrance of Upton in Sophia's mind and the present position of Lady Bellaston in his life present in Tom's. Partridge's indiscretion in talking of Sophia also bulks large in her mind, and shows her sensitivity. He proposes, is moved by her plight to say that he will not ruin her, and both are interrupted by the dramatic arrival of Lady Bellaston. She and Tom are now forced to act a part, with Lady Bellaston suspecting that Sophia is deeper than she appears to be. Tom turns the situation to his advantage, thus showing that he is becoming well-versed in the worldly ways of society.

young booby squire i.e. a simpleton, ignorant of the ways of the world.

Chapter 12

Sophia keeps up her act of not knowing Tom in front of Lady Bellaston, but is outmanouevred by the more experienced woman and does really unconsciously reveal her inclinations. Being Sophia, though, she is not pleased with having been playing at deception anyway.

The elegant Lord Shaftesbury . . . In his 'An Essay on the freedom of wit and humour'.
fibbing i.e. lying.
raillery Joking, mockery.

Revision questions on Book 13

1 Compare and contrast Lady Bellaston and Mrs Fitzpatrick.

2 Write an essay on Mrs Miller, her family and the affair of her cousin.

3 Show how Tom adapts himself to London life and comment on the morality of his position.

4 Show how Fielding makes dramatic use of the unexpected in certain situations in this Book.

Book 14

Chapter 1

This is a calculated defence of learning, and once more provides an excuse for an attack on those critics who deride it. Fielding believes that a writer should know about the subject on which he writes, and if he is writing about life he should certainly know something of that. 'The picture must be after nature herself.' He attacks current society more for its follies than for its vices.

Pitt William Pitt (1708–78) later Earl of Chatham, Prime Minister celebrated for his eloquence.
Demosthenes Athenian statesman and orator (384–22 BC).
Byssh's *Art of Poetry* Published in 1702, a manual or guide to writing.
Quam quisque . . . Let everyone develop the talent that he knows he possesses.
clubbed Combined.
Mr Essex A well-known dancing-master of the time.
Mr Broughton . . . athletics Broughton was a champion boxer.
Titian and Vandyke Two famous painters, the first ?1490–1576 Italian painter of the Venetian school noted for his religious subjects; the second 1599–1641, Flemish-born artist who became court painter to Charles I.
rout A society evening assembly.
What Mr Pope says of women . . . *Moral Essays*, 2 ('Most women have no characters at all.')
Beau Monde Fashionable society.

Chapter 2

The letter from Lady Bellaston shows how much she is taken with Tom and how unpredictable she is, each 'P.S.' being a mark of her neurosis. Then her sudden appearance adds to the drama; then Partridge arrives with Mrs Honour. We now approach farce, as Lady Bellaston hides behind the bed, and Honour abuses her. Tom does his best to offset the effect of this, and Honour ensures that this time he pays her. Tom then has to placate Lady Bellaston, which he just succeeds in doing, though her jealousy towards Sophia is frightful.

was contented . . . another woman had the reversion i.e. she is happy to possess Jones sexually, though she knows that Sophia has his heart.

Chapter 3

A desperate letter from Sophia, and another worrying one from Lady Bellaston, shows that Tom is beset both sexually and romantically. In addition Mrs Miller gives him a kindly warning about his conduct with the ladies, in her house, since she does not wish to acquire a bad reputation. Partridge reveals his lack of tact in having spoken of the robbery, but his reported exchange with Mrs Honour is an amusing one.

Job The Old Testament patriarch.
her chairmen i.e. those who carried her there, here gossip about her.
as sure as ten pence i.e. for certain (ten pence = 4p decimal currency today, but worth much more then).
infandum . . . Beyond all words, O Queen, is the grief you ask me to recall.

Chapter 4

Nightingale, intent on fleeing from love – and note Tom's morality on behalf of him, a morality which he has difficulty in applying to himself. He shows how sympathetic he is towards Nancy. He gives Nightingale a lecture on the irresponsibility of his conduct towards her, distinguishing between his own lust and the fact that he would not injure anybody who was vulnerable. Nightingale responds, but a short account of his character shows that he boasts of his conquests in love.

nice Particular.
Pallmall A fashionable part of London.
make love to her i.e. show that you love her.
not apply them i.e. not take account of your looks?
When ev'ry eye was closed . . . A quotation from a play by Nicholas Rowe called *The Fair Penitent* (1703).

Chapter 5

Mrs Miller tells Tom about Allworthy, now that she knows he is related to the Squire. Again note the technique of the tale, the story within the main story. The motive here is clearly to give a further instance of Allworthy's goodness of heart. Jones is so moved by Mrs Miller's account that he confides in her. Later he waits for Lady Bellaston, tension being aroused in the reader when she does not appear.

a season i.e. a period of time.

Chapter 6

Jones shows his sympathy by spending much time worrying about Mrs Miller's daughter Nancy. He has every cause to, for when he wakes up late he does so to the family drama. Partridge is flippant about it, but not so Tom, who promises to exert himself on the family's behalf. It is a touching scene.

there is a child coming for the Foundling-Hospital i.e. Nancy's child by Nightingale will be put into the orphanage.
taking on Becoming upset.

Chapter 7

Nightingale's conscience certainly bothers him, and the dialogue with Tom reveals that he does love the girl. Tom brings all his influence and sympathy to bear, and persists in using the word 'honour', to stress that Nightingale should marry Nancy. He offers to intercede with Nightingale's father, and Nightingale, who has a cunning streak in him, urges Tom to tell his father that he, Nightingale, is already married.

in the spleen i.e. in a worse mood.

Chapter 8

Fielding ironically defines Mr Nightingale senior as a man of the world. He is ruled by money, a reflection on a number of characters in the novel and many in the real world. Again there is the element of mistaken identity, at first with the father mistaking who Tom is, and then mistaking the subject of their conversation, which is, of course Nancy. The revelation of the supposed marriage brings down his condemnation. The appearance of the brother who is himself trying to marry his daughter to someone she doesn't want shows that the chapter is a lecture on misguided parents.

the Roman satyrist Juvenal, *Satire*, 10.
Seneca In *Epistulae Morales*.
Cicero In *Tusculan Disputations*.
declined Turned away from.
lose his labour i.e. was wasting his time.
banter i.e. play around with me.
St Anthony won upon the fishes St Anthony (1195–1231) so charmed the fish with his eloquence that they leapt out of the water to hear him better.
Orpheus and Amphion Orpheus charmed rocks and trees, Amphion made the stones move into place in the wall of Thebes.

Chapter 9

All appears happy, the uncle goes back to the Miller family with Tom, but his nephew and Nancy feel guilty at the mention of their supposed marriage. There is a deft dramatic stroke when Nightingale has the honesty to admit the truth and has to endure the about-face of his uncle, who tells him to get rid of Nancy. All the while he is complacent that his own daughter will obey him – this in itself is ironic.

ply'd i.e. supplied.
enured Accustomed.

Chapter 10

All is now under suspicion as Nightingale goes off with his uncle, but the tension switches with Mrs Honour's arrival and her dreadful but as yet unrevealed news of Sophia.

Revision questions on Book 14

1 Indicate the part played by letters in this Book.

2 Compare and contrast the characters of Mrs Miller and Nightingale.

3 Write an essay on either the use of retrospect or the influence of money in these chapters.

4 'Tom has double standards.' Discuss this judgement in the light of events in this Book.

Book 15

Chapter 1

A discussion of vice and virtue, very brief, but very telling in its emphasis on both being relative to human nature.

Chapter 2

The revenge of Lady Bellaston on Sophia for presuming to stand between herself and Tom is a consummate piece of hypocrisy. She schemes to get Fellemar into Sophia's company, and gives him all the information he needs and the encouragement to propose to her. She also tells him of his rival and of Sophia's obstinacy, but her luring him to the meal is a calculated piece of opportunism, since her plans run deep.

computation i.e. calculating time.
O brave An exclamation, here meaning 'How wonderful!'
hath you i.e. has enchanted you.
entered the lists i.e. as in a tournament, taken him on, competed with him.

Chapter 3

Fielding's ironic presentation of the *Little World*, a kind of sick practical-joke club. The scheme to see the reactions of Sophia when Tom is mentioned as having been killed shows the level of their 'humour' and of their morality. Lady Bellaston is unscrupulous, Lord Fellemar has a conscience, and the plan of rape is in abeyance in his mind.

the late war That of the Austrian Succession, peace being concluded at Aix-la-Chapelle in October 1748.
a fib . . . vent A lie which he was to circulate.
their rubbers i.e. of whist.
huddling up i.e. promoting.
the ravished Sophia The use of the prophetic epithet indicates Lady Bellaston's plan for Sophia.
Between the acting of a dreadful thing . . . Brutus's words in *Julius Caesar*, Act 2, Scene 1, 63–9.

Chapter 4

By mockery, raillery, Lady Bellaston succeeds in prevailing upon Lord Fellemar to change his mind. Fielding delights in the literary analogies, and Lady Bellaston proves that she is one too many for Fellemar.

Newgate solicitors i.e. those handling criminal cases and who are themselves unscrupulous.
cordial i.e. a pick me up, something to give him courage.
Helen . . . Paris Helen of Troy, wife of Menelaus, who was carried off by Paris. The result was the siege of Troy.
the Sabine ladies They were carried off by the Romans but when their husbands returned the women placed themselves between the ravishers and their husbands.
rather dull when related at second hand Fine irony at the expense of society gossip.

Chapter 5

Notice that, even in his detail here, Fielding has Sophia reading an appropriately titled play. The exchange with Lord Fellemar is full of excitement, but the unexpected arrival of Western is dramatic and opportune. The description of Sophia and Fellemar is grotesque in the aftermath of their struggle; Western, who is drunk, contributes to this. Supple is as sycophantic as ever. Lady Bellaston shows her cunning yet again by wilfully mistaking Western's remarks and virtually helping him to carry off Sophia, so that she is out of the way for her own intrigues.

The Fatal Marriage (1694) By Thomas Southerne (1659–1746).
raise the family i.e. make everybody hear.
unkennel her Notice the image – this could only come from Western.
myrmidons Followers or henchman, originally a race of people whom Zeus made from a nest of ants.
the bag of his wig i.e. the snood which held the hair.
wot ha' un Will have him.
gee you a living with a pox Obscene, meaning 'I won't give you a living at all'.
spit Sword.
lick thy jacket i.e. give you a hiding.
grannum Grandmother.

Chapter 6

The sycophantic letter from Mrs Fitzpatrick to Squire Western's sister, which gives Sophia away. There is an inevitable quarrel and reconciliation between brother and sister, but this is another example of Fielding's use of retrospect, and the squire does not employ the diplomacy his sister suggests; he is in fact incapable of it.

Lewis the fourteenth was at the gates of Amsterdam ... Louis XIV
(1643–1715) besieged the Dutch in Amsterdam in 1672–3. He had to
abandon the siege because the dykes were broken and flooded the land.
Size Assizes.
je vous mesprise ... I despise you with all my heart.
Greenland ... Tramontane negotiation i.e. negotiations with
barbarians.

Chapter 7

Now we return to Mrs Honour's arrival at Mrs Miller's with the bad news about Sophia. She is hysterical, and will not stop talking. With the arrival of Lady Bellaston the earlier farcical scene is reenacted, with Honour being hidden. This is a great embarrassment to Tom, since Lady Bellaston obviously wants him to make love to her. The farce continues with the timely arrival of the drunken Nightingale. It is noticeable that here the women stick together – Honour comes under the influence of Lady Bellaston – while Tom is further exposed by his affair with that lady.

I perceive your distemper i.e. you could have come to see me if you had
wanted to.
Adonis Greek youth noted for his beauty.
Cicero ... Maciavel See earlier notes on p.53 and p.58.
for very made i.e. for speaking too soon.
I constructions i.e. I draw conclusions, make judgements.

Chapter 8

More retrospect, this time on Nightingale's escape from his uncle and the latter's daughter's escape from him by marrying the young clergyman. Nightingale is married to Nancy, Tom being made very happy by his role in bringing about their happiness.

Doctors Commons Ecclesiastical court where marriage licences were
obtained.

Homo sum ... I am myself a man, and have an interest in the concerns of all other men.

complexion Temperament.

Chapter 9

The vacillating nature of Lady Bellaston revealed by her first letter, and her character revealed to Tom by Nightingale. The latter opens up, and Fiedling ironically and discreetly does not tell us the extent of Lady Bellaston's debauchery. Yet Tom has a sense of loyalty towards her. Nightingale's ingenuity in suggesting that Tom propose to her seems an attractive way out, but it is fraught with difficulties. It is an important plot pivot.

the queen of the fairies i.e. Lady Bellaston thus styled herself in her invitation to Tom to the masquerade.

nicety Delicacy.

vestal kind i.e. a virgin.

he gave a lattitude ... i.e. he encouraged him to speak.

the future commentators on our works Fielding is ever ironic about his own writing.

wanted a bit of bread i.e. starved.

his commerce i.e. his relationship.

handsome pretence i.e. a convincing argument.

declare off before the knot is ty'd i.e. withdraw before you have to marry her.

his privy-council Note how subtly Fielding manages to keep up his running political innuendo.

Chapter 10

Allworthy coming to town, and the embarrassment this causes to Mrs Miller, is offset by Tom's willingness to move, though he himself is apprehensive at the thought of the coming visit. He is also worried about Sophia, since Honour has not been in touch with him. When she does send him a wonderfully comic letter without spelling or grammar, she tells him the doubtful news that she is now in the employ of Lady Bellaston.

requite so disinterested i.e. repay Nightingale for marrying Nancy.

Beyond the fixed and settled rules The opening lines of 'Paulo Purganti and His Wife' by Matthew Prior (1664–1721).

Addison says of Caesar ... In his play *Cato* (1713).

verbatim and literatim Word for word and letter for letter.

I shud sartenly haf kaled ... I should certainly have called (now translate the rest of what Mrs Honour says).

Chapter 11

More letters, this time an extraneous incident being involved, the love of Mrs Hunt for Tom, her delicate way of putting it, his loyalty to Sophia despite his now near poverty – all this provides an interlude of a chapter. It shows that Tom, however, has developed in character.

old Turkey merchant i.e. engaged in trade with the Turkish empire.
billet Letter.
dunned i.e. forced to pay up.
scrutore Desk.

Chapter 12

Partridge proves his usefulness and the plot takes another turn with the discovery of Black George, who is now working as a servant with the Western family. With the impending arrival of Blifil and the marriage plans being laid there is tension before Tom begins to write to Sophia.

infinitive . . . imperative i.e. you would be at the end before we have established the beginning.
Non sum qualis eram I am not what I was (from Horace).
ad unguem To a finger nail (i.e. accurately).
my charmer Current term for the beloved, the person who is loved.

Revision questions on Book 15

1 Write a character study of Lady Bellaston as she appears in this Book.

2 'Deception is at the heart of Fielding's matter in *Tom Jones*.' Do you agree or disagree with this statement.

3 Write an essay on love in this Book.

4 Which do you consider to be the most dramatic incident in this Book and why?

Book 16

Chapter 1

An ironic commentary on the nature of prologues and his own free employment of them before each book, together with another snipe at the critics, who will always find matter to censure in the prologues.

pate Head.
emolument Payment.
a whetstone to his noble spirit [Sarcasm] Spur him on to write critically.

Chapter 2

The scene shifts to Mr Western's lodgings. The squire's cruel treatment of Sophia is seen in his leaving her alone there for about thirty-six hours. The arrival of the genteel gentleman and the comic effect produced on Western by the idea of a duel (the humour lies in his misunderstanding the language) is followed by his scene with Sophia. Remember that he has already been humiliated by the assault, but he shows no compassion for Sophia's state, even when she promises that she will never marry Tom.

baggage-waggons JPs had to issue warrants to constables for the provision of baggage waggons when troops were on the march.
they are a parcel of courtiers . . . Note that the squire's prejudices remain the same in town.
refuse him satisfaction i.e. either to apologize or to fight a duel with him.
manual remonstrances . . . i.e. he boxed his ears.
single stick i.e. with a stick held in one hand by each of the combatants.
At unt If you are.
a brass varden i.e. no money at all (not give a brass farthing).
choused Tricked.
shat unt You won't.
the turnkey of Newgate The gaoler of that terrible prison.
a bawd i.e. a procuress for prostitution.

Chapter 3

The conveying of Tom's letter in an egg to Sophia is done with consummate humour and literary analogy. Tom's letter is a mixture of desire that she should run away with him and the opposite, that she should give him up. There is the usual note of expectation at the end of the chapter with the noise of the arrival of Mrs Western.

hastish Impetuous.
Bansted Banstead; noted for the fresh air.
the Royal Society Founded in 1660, and often satirized by Fielding for the attention it gave to freaks of nature.
Ovid . . . Hyacinthus *Metamorphoses*, 10, where Hyacinthus was killed and his blood was changed into flowers, on the leaves of which the word 'Woe' appeared ('Ai' in Greek).
maw Belly.
academies des sciences i.e. learned scientific societies.
a round bout i.e. a real quarrel or fight.

Chapter 4

To the surprise of Western, he is attacked by his sister for the imprisonment of Sophia, but that strong-minded lady, a prototype feminist, will have none of this, for she has her own ambitions for Sophia. The abject situation of Sophia is given a considered stress, and we note that she is really a plaything between the squire and his sister.

turnpike acts i.e. passed for the improvement of roads, and thus demanding higher tolls of the public who used them.
Thalestris See note Book 9, Chapter 3.
whip thee in Typical language of hunting for the squire to use.
with a full ratification Typical too of Mrs Western – the language of wars and treaties.
muore More.
medicinal julap i.e. liquor, which has the effect of curing him of his temper (temporarily).
capuchin A cloak with a hood, like that of a monk.
should have taken a dance thru the horse-pond Western means that he would have pitched him into it.

Chapter 5

Sophia reveals that she is honourable in her promises, tells Tom that he must write no more, and encloses the bank-bill for him. Tom's reactions of grief and joy are predictable. The visit to the theatre to see *Hamlet* is cause for humour because of the running commentary of Partridge. In a sense it is a mockery of those who go to plays and don't understand what they see. Partridge preferring the King to the other characters is a master-stroke.

That refined degree of Platonic affection i.e. an ideal rather than a fleshly love.
the Common-Prayer Book . . . Treason service The plot to blow up

Parliament on 5 November 1605 was remembered in the Prayer book of
1745 by the portrait of a man with a lantern approaching the doors of
Parliament.

Garrick David Garrick (1717–79); famous English actor, manager and
dramatist.

Follow you Partridge is of course echoing the text of the play.

Nulla fides fronti There is no trusting appearances (*Juvenal*).

Nemo omnibus horis sapit No one is always wise.

Chapter 6

Charming introduction, with the author regarding all his characters
as his children. Blifil is informed that Sophia is found, his emphasis on
his hatred is brought to our notice, together with his hypocrisy to
Allworthy, who has to be reassured that Blifil is very much in love
with Sophia before he will agree to let the marriage go ahead.

Chapter 7

The tactlessness of Western in bringing Blifil straight to Sophia is
stressed, but Blifil is suspicious of Mrs Western's attitude and, as the
author observes, he is right to be so.

matrimonial politics Good phrase to describe Mrs Western's appraisal of
the situation.

recruit Raise.

contexture i.e. mixture of feelings and emotions.

I can no more turn her . . . Hunting term again – I can no more bring her
to my way of thinking.

Chapter 8

An important chapter in the sense that it contains (a) Lady Bellaston's idea that Tom should be impressed into the Navy and thus got
away from the scene, leaving Lord Fellemar in the clear for Sophia
and (b) the passing on of Tom's letter of proposal to Lady Bellaston.
This ensures that Mrs Western will be able to blackmail Sophia. Of
surpassing interest is the fact that since both these ladies are intent on
serving Lord Fellemar, they will come into direct collision with Squire
Western.

pressed and sent on board a ship Impressment had always been
practised, but in 1744 an act was passed which extended the practice and
gave local authorities the power to take such action.

a carte blanche i.e. complete freedom.
a Hottentot A savage (a reference to Tom).

Chapter 9

Mrs Fitzpatrick has already been treated badly by Squire Western and his sister, and has consequently changed her attitude towards Tom. Her suggestion that he approach Mrs Western and propose to her is a petty attempt at revenge, but Mrs Fitzpatrick is herself susceptible, and flirts openly with Tom.

scurvy compellations i.e. insulting remarks.
liquorish i.e. lecherous.
Oroondates The hero of a romance by La Calprenede called *Cassandre* (1644–50).
which we don't care to convey ... Fielding perfectly understands the art of reticence that suggests more by implication than revelation.

Chapter 10

The jealousy of Mrs Fitzpatrick is now brought to the fore again. Tom is guiltless and friendly when Fitzpatrick sees him emerge from Mrs Fitzpatrick's house. The fight, the wounding of Fitzpatrick, the sudden eruption of men who seize Tom, all is done with graphic immediacy. Tom's being taken to prison is likewise sudden, the surgeon's news that Mr Fitzpatrick will not survive is suspicious (since we know what Fielding thinks of surgeons), and Sophia's letter is the unkindest cut of all. Lady Bellaston's poison has done its work.

knock over the pate A blow on the head.
he hath prevented his voyage ... i.e. we cannot impress him, for he will be charged with murder and will not be able to go.
the Gate-house Main prison in Westminster.

Revision questions on Book 16

1 Write an essay of appreciation on the visit to the theatre.

2 Who do you consider the most evil, Lady Bellaston or Mrs Fitzpatrick? Give reasons for your answer.

3 In what ways does the author make his moral views clear during these chapters? Refer to the text in your answer.

Book 17

Chapter 1

The author ponders on the hard task he has given himself in having to extricate his characters from trouble before the end of the novel. At the same time, he teases the reader by implying (but obviously not believing) that Tom will come to a bad end. There is a short digression on the way the ancient writers handled events through reference to the gods or genii.

a few moral sentences Note the irony of the phrase.
felo de se 'Felons to themselves.' The legal term for suicides.
taking a first row at Tyburn i.e. to see the 'performance' of a hanging.
delivering i.e. rescuing.

Chapter 2

Blifil reveals his malice towards Tom by recounting the story of his killing a man, and Mrs Miller shows her generosity of spirit by warmly defending Tom to Allworthy. The latter is surprised that he even knows Tom, but as yet he is unrelenting.

the devil marks his best beloved i.e. shows that he is evil.

Chapter 3

Western's battle with the chairmen shows that he resents London and considers that all Londoners are intent on swindling. His report of the society gathering and the mincing ways of the town is pure comedy. Allworthy shows his decency in refusing to have any part in forcing Sophia, and his praise of her shows a true appreciation of her worth (though she has convinced him that she is a woman who will entirely subordinate herself to men's judgement). Allworthy goes so far, in his humane attitude towards marriage, to decline the match; but Blifil wishes to persevere, and although Allworthy thinks this perseverance is a 'vulgar error', the intention is to go ahead.

Brown Bess Mr Western's horse.
a fox ... a badger Tom ... Lord Fellamar.
My land ... Hannover Expressive of the Squire's fear of the nobles and the court being in the power of the King.
hoop-petticoat See note p.92.

Acton i.e. Acteon, who saw Diana bathing, whereupon she turned him into
a stag and he was torn to pieces by his hounds.

clap back Crouch down in the position of a hare.

zeed half oum i.e. saw half of them.

Doctors Commons See note p.101.

a highest deference . . . a quality absolutely essential Allworthy,
despite his general enlightenment and humanity, shows himself to be
somewhat chauvinistic here.

shat ha her i.e. you shall have her.

gee Give.

any countenance i.e. any encouragement.

Chapter 4

A digression about Nature, which relates to Sophia's situation –
before we plunge into her argument with her aunt, which shows that
aunt's ambitions with regard to Fellemar. But Sophia shows not only
an independence of spirit but also a degree of cunning that we might
not have expected. She so flatters Mrs Western as to put her in a good
mood and thus Fellemar is frustrated when he arrives. The aunt has
so much vanity that she reflects upon her own love affairs rather than
promoting her niece's at this stage.

Parthenissa The chaste heroine of a romance by the Earl of Orrery
(1621–79).

Tully Cicero In his *Epistulae ad Familiares*.

Chapter 5

Mrs Miller's generous action in determining to visit Tom is complemented by a digression on constancy in friendship. Tom is oppres-
sed at the thought of having shed the blood of another human being.
Mrs Miller undertakes to further help Tom by delivering the letter to
Sophia. Nightingale is intent upon the truth about Fitzpatrick, and
the chapter demonstrates the qualities of friendship.

The black ingredient . . . envy One of the most directly overt moral
statements in the novel.

would stand you for a shilling i.e. would take your place for a shilling
(5p, but worth much more then).

Chapter 6

Mrs Miller's determination to tell Sophia everything relating to
Tom's goodness produces an effect on that at first adamant young

lady. When she reads the letter Sophia, in her innocence and naiveté, can make nothing of the Lady Bellaston proposal, though she has to endure the latter's insults. There follows a finely satirical account of a drum.

Chapter 7

Mrs Miller upsets Allworthy somewhat for, having confided in him with regard to Tom's goodness, she contrives to cast aspersions on the character and motives of Blifil. Allworthy here reveals how wrong-headed he can be, though he agrees to try to reconcile old Mr Nightingale to the match. The arrival of Dowling suggests some movement in the plot.

Chapter 8

The interview between Sophia and Lord Fellamar shows Sophia's spirit, and there is the now customary eavesdropping (here by Mrs Western), which ensures that she has no privacy. In any case Mrs Western has had Mrs Miller betrayed to her and has pumped her of all information, so that Sophia is completely beset.

a comb-brush i.e. attending to her mistress's personal needs.
procuress i.e. getting girls for prostitution.
the wise King of Prussia Frederick the Great (1712–84) signed peace treaties with the other nations in order to carry on the war more effectively against France.

Chapter 9

The researches of Nightingale seems to have drawn a blank, and this chapter consists of a succession of appearances, the last of these, Mrs Waters, being dramatic. There is retrospect on her relationship with Mr Fitzpatrick and coincidence is stretched to the utmost here. There is a complete about-turn, for Mrs Waters brings the direct news that Mr Fitzpatrick is not in mortal danger. Tom is still tormented by thoughts of Sophia.

rencounter i.e. incident in which Fitzpatrick was wounded.
hedge-tavern A low and disreputable pub.
a Throne still greatly superior i.e. that of God, in Heaven.
the safest seconds i.e. supporters.
pinked Wounded.
the Devil when he was sick From Rabelais The devil was sick, the devil a monk would be, the devil was well, the devil a monk was he.

Revision questions on Book 17

1 In what ways do you find the plot in this Book contrived? Give reasons for your answer.

2 'Allworthy is too good to be true.' Discuss this statement in the light of this Book.

3 Write an essay of appreciation of Fielding's use of dialogue, with reference to two chapters in this Book.

Book 18

Chapter 1

The comparison of the novel to a stage-coach journey is a good one, particularly in view of the number of inns we have visited. Fielding jokes about how much he has to cram into this final book, and protests that he has not meant to offend anyone.

jest-sake personated i.e. for the sake of the joke.
If in anything I have offended . . . An echo of Feste at the end of *Twelfth Night*.

Chapter 2

Fielding now threatens to become a sensation novelist with the (supposed) revelations that Mrs Waters is Tom's mother and that he has slept with her. Tom blames himself for his own 'folly and vice'. Again there is misunderstanding when Black George arrives, but his function is to report the row between Western and his sister that has led to a partial reconciliation with Sophia.

you have been a-bed with your own mother Note the bluntness of the statement.
Billingsgate i.e. the use of extremely bad language.

Chapter 3

The narrative now moves quickly, with the discovery of the bank-notes and the crime of Black George. Allworthy tells Mrs Miller of his real affection for Tom, and the good news continues when Nightingale arrives. We notice that the narrative points now in the direction of reconciliation between Tom and Allworthy, through coincidence and through the good offices of their friends.

gamesters Gamblers.
the Black Act An Act (1723) against deer-stalkers and poachers who blackened their faces and tried to extort money by blackmail.

Chapter 4

Once more the use of letters to convey information, this time a moving one from Square which contains his confession of the wrong he has done to Tom. It is balanced by the Thwackum letter with its totally uncharitable and arrogant emphasis.

Plato himself concludes his *Phaedon* *Phaedon* 107b,114d.
pluralities i.e. holding more than one living.

Chapter 5

The appearance of Dowling leads to further revelations, particularly when Allworthy interrogates Nightingale. Blifil's hypocrisy is manifest to Mrs Miller, but not to Allworthy. Partridge is seen by Allworthy, and tension is raised by the fact that he may reveal what he believes is Tom's incest.

conquered rebellion . . . government . . . A direct reference to the putting down of the Jacobite revolt.

Chapter 6

The attempt to establish who is Tom's father through another retrospective narrative, this time from Partridge. He tells Allworthy of Mrs Waters, but the real drama of the chapter comes with the appearance of that lady herself.

15s to 301 i.e. about 75p to £30, the latter a vast sum of money.
Size i.e. the local assizes.

Chapter 7

The revelations continue, with Mrs Waters, formerly Jenny Jones, giving Allworthy the history of the birth of his sister's child by the

parson Summer and also of the activities supposedly in his name
against Tom.

wave i.e. ignore, forget, dismiss.

Chapter 8

The narrative pace of this final book is dependent on revelations and
incidents. Allworthy now wishes to see Sophia and, more particularly,
Dowling, but Mrs Waters testifies to the goodness of Tom and how he
saved her from the villain Northerton. Dowling, in Mrs Waters'
presence, is virtually compelled to reveal to Allworthy the nefarious
plot of Blifil against Tom. He also reveals of course Mrs Blifil's last
words which Blifil should have told his uncle – that Tom was really his
nephew. The climax of the chapter is masterly – Allworthy shows
Blifil that he knows what he has done.

What the devil and Dr Faustus From the proverbial expression 'as great
  as the devil and Dr Faustus'. The latter, in Marlowe's play, sells his soul to
  the devil.
dree Three.
meet with worse meat i.e. do worse for himself.
no' orow Not any other.
council Lawyer.
trover The offence of finding and keeping the property of another, i.e.
  'stealing through finding'.
subornation of perjury Inducing another person to tell lies.
a lie in the words of truth A finely economical coinage.

Chapter 9

Allworthy shows his consideration for Sophia, and she in return
behaves modestly, as we should expect, and with an indication of her
integrity. The revelations continue, and Allworthy now becomes the
advocate of Tom with Sophia. Strangely, she says that she cannot
admit the thought of marrying Tom, since she is concerned on her
father's account and could only marry with his consent. Paradoxi-
cally, Sophia continues to praise Tom. Western makes his usual
dramatic entrance, but once he realizes that Tom is to be made
Allworthy's heir, he changes his tune and the way is prepared for the
young lovers.

I have hit o't I have discovered the truth.
along o' zister i.e. because of my sister's influence.

Chapter 10

The moving reconciliation between Tom and Allworthy, with the latter reading a moral and Christian lecture despite his own suffering on Tom's account. As usual, though, Allworthy has misread Sophia's reactions, and Tom suffers the more now that he is on the edge of rejection. Mrs Miller reinforces Allworthy's account of Sophia with her own. Western's tune, as we have said, is now completely changed, and he is obviously unaware of his own hypocrisy in thus welcoming Tom and treating him as if he were already engaged to Sophia.

inditing Writing.
I took thee for another person This is ambiguous – what he means is that he took him to be a bastard, but such niceties elude Western.
a't as hearty an honest cock i.e. as straight and strong a young man . . .
litigation i.e. discussion, argument.

Chapter 11

The noble behaviour of Fellamar occupies the first part of this chapter, with retrospect again employed in this account of Tom's release. Tom then counsels his uncle to be generous in his treatment of Blifil, visits Blifil and behaves kindly to him, though the latter is abject in his reactions, and then also asks his uncle to forgive Black George when the story of the bank-notes is told.

remarkably mean i.e. abject, servile.

Chapter 12

Tom and Sophia brought together to advantage, though a little undermined by the coarseness of Western's comments. Tom pleads eloquently for himself, while Sophia is strong and independent in her assertion that time alone is the true judge of penitence. But she gives way, particularly after some flattery, and Western returns, having heard it all – inevitably – to bring about the marriage the next day. Allworthy is joyful, Western coarsely anticipatory of a grandson nine months to the day.

sha't ha' the tousling her i.e. have her sexually.
on the security i.e. the guarantee.
Dorimant, Lord Rochester Dorimant is the dissolute hero of *The Man of Mode* (1676) by Sir John Etherege, while Rochester was also something of a libertine.

O transporting thought i.e. I am uplifted by the idea.
That's it, little honeys . . . Language he would use to his dogs.
flimflam Nonsense.
And wunt nut ha un And won't you have him . . .
thou at a puppy i.e. you're not bold enough.
minding other matters Paying attention to other things.
Hast nut gin i.e. haven't you given.
a crown i.e five shillings (25p).
wut ha? What will you have?

Chapter The Last

Reconciliation is the theme, starting with old Nightingale, his conten-
tious brother, and their children, though old Nightingale still broods
on the loss of a fortune that might have been his son's lot in marriage.
There is a nice touch in the preferment of Mr Abraham Adams, the
unworldly and infinitely loveable parson of Fielding's earlier novel,
Joseph Andrews. The one surprising twist to the happy endings is the
marriage of Mrs Waters and Parson Supple.

palliate Lessen.
sat in his cups i.e. continued drinking heavily.
purchase a seat . . . In the days before free elections seats in Parliament
  could be purchased, hence Blifil's saving.
on foot i.e. in the offing.

Revision questions on Book 18

1 Write an essay on the most interesting revelations that occur in
these chapters.

2 How far do the happy endings undermine the realism of *Tom
Jones*?

3 'Christian morality is at the heart of Fielding's art.' How far do
you agree or disagree with this statement?

Fielding's Art in *Tom Jones*
The Characters

Tom Jones

. . . they are the faults of wildness and of youth . . . they are vastly overbalanced by one of the most humane tender honest hearts that ever man was blessed with.

Mrs Miller's words given above aptly define the main elements of Tom's character. Our first introduction to him shows him to be loyal, obstinate and brave, again qualities that are to be demonstrated throughout his life. Here he conceals Black George's part in the trespass, but is so moved by Allworthy's concern (he gives Tom a horse as a present) that he nearly confesses everything. This shows the generosity and warmth of his nature. Fielding's presentation of character means that the author's voice is often employed in mitigation of actions, so that we know that Tom, named as the hero, will certainly turn out right in the end. We feel the weight of the author's sympathetic identification with his creature. Tom, though brutalized by Thwackum after the manner of the times, never becomes brutal in his own actions and reactions. In some ways he is too good to be true, for instance in his early love for Blifil, though he gives him a bloody nose on one occasion when Blifil refers to him as a *'beggarly bastard'*.

This indicates another aspect of Tom's character, namely his impetuosity, which, as he grows up and becomes a young man, develops into sexual opportunism, as with Molly Seagrim and the still attractive Mrs Waters. Tom has strong feelings for others, witness his responsibilities to Black George's family even before he falls in love with Molly. Tom's outgoing nature means that he becomes popular with the servants and the people of the neighbourhood. There is an independence in his nature that often turns into rudeness.

What Fielding calls Tom's 'gallantry of temper' recommends him to his unknown mother and to women generally throughout the narrative. Although reluctant to nurture bitterness, he does vow revenge on Thwackum for the way he treats him. We note more readily his goodness of nature, seen in his selling the Bible and the horse to provide for Black George's family. He loves hunting, and in this way and without effort ingratiates himself with Squire Western. He has a natural gaiety of temper which recommends him to the young Sophia, but the bird incident shows his courage and anticipates his devotion to her. There is a degree of innocence about him, particularly in relation to Sophia, and, though this may appear paradoxical, with regard to Molly Seagrim, where his feelings pass from love to a kind of protective attitude which never entirely leaves him, as we see at the end of the novel. He believes that he is the father of Molly's child (he is romantic and a little naive here) and confesses to Allworthy that he has corrupted her. He saves Sophia from falling but injures his arm in doing so, though when she has visited him during his confinement he realizes that he loves her. Since he is already devoted to Molly he determines to think no more of Sophia, but this is impossible. Again his naiveté is in evidence when he tries to give Molly money, but this gives way to mirth when he finds that she is having an affair with the philosopher Square. Tom has a good sense of humour, and rather likes Square the more for being human and compromised. We also suspect that there is some relief in his attitude, for he counsels Molly to be faithful to Square, thus freeing himself from her.

In Sophia's company Fielding has Tom, a man of spirit, behave like the conventional romantic hero who becomes tongue-tied and trembling because of the presence of the beloved. This is meant to show his sensitivity, but it is the most unconvincing aspect of his otherwise full-blooded character. He comes much more alive during Allworthy's supposedly near-fatal illness. Here his gratitude for the legacy contrasts tellingly with the reactions of the others present who are treated more than generously. When Blifil tells Allworthy the news of his sister's death Tom is angry, but that anger translates itself to unrestrained joy when he realizes that Allworthy is not going to die. He celebrates in his own way by drinking too much, an action that is used effectively but unfairly against him later. Blifil's narrow-mindedness brings out the irascible aspect of Tom's character, though he cools down; it is true to say that he never lets his pride stand in the way of reconciliation.

Caught with Molly – after expressing his love for Sophia – Tom shows his physical strength in laying low Blifil and belabouring Thwackum, then saves Sophia. But his romantic adoration is overthrown by the determination of the Squire and his sister that Sophia shall marry Blifil. Tom, hitherto made much of by the Squire, finds himself now rejected, despite his supplications. His dismissal by Allworthy follows – for Tom, adversity rarely comes as a single blow – and then he loses the pocket-book which is appropriated by Black George. His only hope at this stage is to be found in the kind letter he receives from Sophia. This is more than balanced by the one from Blifil.

From now on Tom is on the move, reacting impatiently to the

Quaker's story about his daughter, falling in with the soldiers and being uplifted by 'the glorious cause of liberty, and of the Protestant religion'. He decides to serve as a volunteer, but his sincerity, the manner of his conduct, and his lack of experience finds him easy bait for someone like Northerton. Wounded, he displays what we have come to expect from Tom, considerable courage in wanting to fight Northerton and also in enduring the mishandling of the surgeon. With commendable honesty he talks of his own wildness but also of the sincerity of his faith. Tom has a strong personality, and when the sergeant tries to swindle him over the price of the sword he responds so strongly that the other carefully changes the price. When the sentry collapses Tom shows his generosity by asking the officer not to punish the poor man.

He endures with fortitude the insults which his near poverty inevitably provokes, but even at this stage he is resilient enough to be amused by Partridge. What is interesting is the fact that although he has little or no money he has the power of attraction, and this is what moves Partridge to go with him. Tom's function as rescuer receives added opportunities now that he journeys on again; he saves the Man of the Hill from robbers and soon rescues Mrs Waters from Northerton. He shows that he is philosophical in his discussions with the Man of the Hill, also that he has a great deal of faith in human nature. His own nature is readily susceptible to the charms of Mrs Waters, and he succumbs to them. On their discovery by Fitzpatrick, however, he shows his usual resilience and his chivalric concern for the lady.

Tom is out of the action for long periods of the novel once the pursuit of Sophia gets under way. At times he is sore beset by despair over his situation with Sophia, but his resilience serves him well. He guards Sophia's bank-bill as he would guard her honour, and rewards, and promises to reward further, the lame fellow who found it and who becomes so greedy. He is greedy for news of Sophia, and meets Dowling the lawyer. Typically, he confides in the latter and proves that he is without envy. Indeed, so innocent is Tom that he does not realize just how he has been abused with Allworthy. In an argument with Partridge he sticks to his principles in refusing to use Sophia's money. When he encounters the highwayman, instead of being violent and vengeful he shows compassion, and what Fielding says that half his readers will consider an act of 'extraordinary humanity.' He is to be amply repaid later by the man's gratitude and the revelation that he is Mrs Miller's relation.

Tom arrives in London and falls into the trap of the sexually promiscuous Lady Bellaston. We may call his morals in question here, but it would be true to say that he is impoverished, and that Lady Bellaston buys his body but not his heart or soul. Before that Mrs Fitzpatrick bears eloquent testimony to his appeal. Tom rescues Nightingale from his footman, befriends Mrs Miller, ultimately brings Nightingale and Nancy together, relieves the distress of Mrs Miller's relations, and at one stage considers getting rid of Partridge's services because he has no means of supporting that poor fellow. This is probably why Lady Bellaston gets her way with him so easily.

Lady Bellaston's movement towards revenge, however, ends what fleeting happiness he has. Fortune and that lady see him imprisoned after the wounding of Fitzpatrick, the rumours that attend it, and the opportunist action of Blifil against him. Only the kindness and genuine sympathy and actions of his friends sustain him. The visit of Mrs Waters gives him hope, the revelations of Partridge that Mrs Waters is his supposed mother plunges him into despair as he believes he has committed incest. Tom, who is volatile by nature, now feels himself mad. He curses Fortune, but the fickleness of the latter now begins to turn. The revelation that he is Allworthy's real nephew, and of the plot against him, brings Tom right back into favour. He proves to have somewhat more than an ordinarily forgiving nature, overlooking apparently the past coarse condemnations of Western, and intercedes with his uncle over Blifil. He waxes philosophical over Blifil's actions, is kind and considerate to him in his suffering, and only feels disdain when Blifil becomes revoltingly more abject.

His scene with Sophia before she relents is almost too much to take – he is repentant and becomes strikingly lyrical in her company and in praise of her, qualities we have not noticed before. He behaves with becoming modesty on his wedding-day. Tom is a likeable character, full of good humour, toughness, honour, a sense of justice and a developed moral sense. His wildness normalizes him, fate cannot deter him. Although he is often romantically inarticulate where Sophia is concerned we are strongly aware of his virility, animal spirits and kindliness. He is a little larger than life. Refreshingly, he never becomes cloying, and the result is that we respond to his engaging qualities, accept and even like his sins, and tolerate a goodness that sometimes extends beyond the bounds of probability.

Mr Allworthy

an agreeable person, a sound constitution, a solid understanding, and a benevolent heart.

Allworthy is Fielding's ideal man, but he is not so idealized as to be incredible, since because of his benevolence, his tendency to see good and exclude bad, he is often in error and possesses a kind of blindness. This lasts over a period of many years with his nephew Blifil. The first time we really see Allworthy he is in his nightshirt in contemplation of the baby Tom, and in a sense this posture, where he is intent on goodness and unaware of ridicule, is his throughout the novel. He is kind, tolerant, good-natured, compassionate, easily taken advantage of and yet possessing a greater insight than we should at first give him credit for. His loving-kindness to the baby is touching; his memory of his wife more so. His treatment of Jenny is compassionate, though the sermon he reads her is perhaps too long for her – and our – taste. It registers sufficiently with us, however, to underline the strict but warm Christianity of the man. The calumnies against him, for instance that he is the father of the child, do not influence him at all.

Although we are told that 'men of genius and learning shared the principal place in his favour' we note that he is gullible to others of a different caste, notably Captain Blifil, Thwackum and Square, all of whom take advantage of him in their particular ways. He sees through Captain Blifil, but the long regime of Thwackum and Square under-lines his capacity to be too tolerant, even to be misled, and one feels that despite all his goodness Allworthy spends too much of his life being too trusting.

Allworthy shows great understanding and compassion for Tom's errors until he is undermined by deception. He is adept at distin-guishing, on occasions, the specious reasoning of Thwackum and Square. Such is his sense of fairness that he makes up to Blifil when he is the object of his mother's dislike, since Allworthy cannot bear to see anyone wrongly treated. He dislikes it when Tom – though with good reason – threatens revenge against Thwackum. When he realizes the state of deprivation existing in Black George's family he immediately gives them money for food and clothes.

Because *Tom Jones* is a picaresque novel Allworthy is absent from the action for much of the time, but his presence, shown in the reverence that Tom and Mrs Miller hold for him, is never pushed into the moral background of the story. Before Tom is sent away Allworthy is generous in his judgment of him when Tom accuses himself of having corrupted Molly Seagrim. He always does his utmost to bring Tom 'to a sober sense of his indiscreet conduct'. His own illness shows a generosity of fact and spirit which meets with undeserved and insensitive abuse from those for whom he makes provision. He is brave in the face of what he thinks is death, but he has little or no judgement of the reactions of others, little knowing that Thwackum and Square are dissatisfied with their position. Allwor-

thy's response to the news of his sister's death again reflects his
fortitude and courage. It also reflects his faith.

Allworthy's presence in the novel is permanent, and we see this in
Book 14 when Mrs Miller tells Tom of his goodness to her on the death
of her husband. His settling £50 a year on her is a measure of his
practical generosity and concern. When he comes to London he does
so at Blifil's wish in order to see if the match with Sophia can be
genuinely furthered. He listens to Mrs Miller's views on Tom, allows
them to be undercut by Blifil, but refuses to encourage the courtship of
Sophia because he sees that she is averse to Blifil. He counsels the
latter to forego any claim by consulting his heart. At the same time he
allows himself to be ruffled by Mrs Miller's warm partisanship of
Tom, but his visit to old Nightingale and the discovery that Black
George has appropriated the money sets him towards Tom, and the
self-knowledge gradually emerges that he has misjudged him. What
Fielding refers to as 'the visible alteration in Mr Allworthy's mind,
and the abatement of his anger to Jones' now occurs, and his
interrogation of Dowling and Mrs Waters, always with the active
sympathetic participation of Mrs Miller, shows that his past blindness is being dispersed. Square's letter helps as well, for Allworthy as
always is receptive to influences. He is also conditioned by the
warmth of his memories for the little foundling even before he
discovers that Tom is his sister's child.

Allworthy, though having his creator's sympathetic approbation
throughout, is sometimes not only too good to be true but also too true
to be good. But his errors are all on the side of the angels; he acts
always from the best motives, and his genuine qualities, which are so
early spelt out by his creator, endear him to us and make him the most
profoundly Christian presence in the novel.

Squire Western

Drink about . . . Pox of your laws of nature. I don't know what you mean,
either of you by right or wrong.

Sophia's father is hard-hunting, hard-drinking, insensitive and uncultivated. He is largely caricature, but he exerts a powerful influence
in the novel. Like Allworthy, he has lost his wife, but whereas
Allworthy has given himself increasingly to philosophy and Christian
charities, the Squire has let himself go. But there is every evidence
that his tendencies were already well advanced during his marriage.
We are told that his wife was merely a kind of upper servant. Western
is a man of rooted prejudices, hating anything to do with the present
regime and stigmatizing all evils as stemming from the court and the

Hanoverians. His passion, as we have said, is hunting, and even when he goes in pursuit of Sophia that passion takes priority, as when he turns aside to hunt with a squire in the neighbourhood and then returns to his own home.

It would be too simple to say that he cherishes Sophia; perhaps it would be accurate to say that he cherishes her in his own mind. This means subjecting her to his will. In fact, though he can be influenced by Allworthy and more particularly his sister, he is bloody-minded and aggressive whenever he is crossed. Apart from hunting and the bottle, his other interest – if it can be termed such – is his property and the advantages that can be gained from it, the first and foremost being money. Thus the proposal of Blifil for Sophia is most welcome to him – his property is secured within his family and he would acquire Allworthy's property too, or rather Sophia would in terms of her marriage. Western's standards are double ones. He delights in Tom's drinking and sporting company, delights also in his getting a wench with child, tells lies about Allworthy having been promiscuous in his youth when they were together (which they never were), and yet is appalled at the thought of Tom courting his daughter. His hypocrisy is shown by the fact that when Allworthy reveals who Tom is – and that he will be his heir – Western's response is to behave as if nothing had happened and to welcome Tom with open arms.

His arguments with his sister show his liverish irascibility, but they are always made up because neither can bear the thought of being omitted from the other's will. His treatment of Sophia is degrading to the name of humanity, his insistence that she shall have a man she cannot tolerate expressive of the ultimate in domestic tyranny. He is violent (witness one scene with Tom and his assault on Lord Fellemar) and has to be restrained; his language fluctuates between the coarse and the obscene, he is ignorant, boorish and unprincipled. There is little doubt that he is caricature, yet one feels that Fielding's acute study of human nature would show him many men of his time like Squire Western.

Blifil

a lad of remarkable disposition; sober, discreet, and pious, beyond his age.

The irony of the above quotation is expressive of Fielding's art in *Tom Jones*. Blifil is a hypocrite, seen in contrast to the generally open Tom (Tom only lies to save others) his weedy unphysicality contrasts markedly with the boisterous and spirited behaviour of his half-brother. As a boy Blifil is a tell-tale, several times landing Tom in trouble. All is done under the guise of goodness, but this is spurious.

Perhaps here the most obvious incident is Blifil's releasing Sophia's bird on the pretext that he did not believe that it should be denied its freedom.

Blifil is a consummate liar, but worse than that, of course, is the fact that he is encouraged to be one. I refer to the influence of Thwackum and Square on his childhood, where he is always right and Tom is always wrong. Thus conditioned – and with the inheritance of his father (a deliberate deceiver) and of his mother (who maintains her deception until just before her death), Blifil's actions do not bear scrutiny. Two other instances of this wilful self-indulgence stand out. The first is that he conceals his mother's letter of confession, thus ensuring his own continuance in Allworthy's favour at the expense of Tom. The second is related to this, in that he reveals his mother's death when Allworthy might be supposed to be at his weakest, and where we feel that Blifil is hopeful of Allworthy's collapse at the reception of the news. Tom suspects this, and Blifil compounds this sin by later distorting Tom's reactions to Allworthy's recovery.

Blifil is not flesh and blood but glibness and hypocrisy personified. His employment of Dowling and his attempts to make sure that Tom is convicted reveal a mean and corrupt mind. That meanness is shown too in his relations with Sophia, where he changes from indifference to hate because of her partiality for Tom and also because of her running away. It never occurs to him to withdraw. As for so many of the characters in *Tom Jones*, for Blifil money speaks louder than honour or morality. He is his father's son down to every little dishonest reflex of action and character. He never really becomes more than caricature, but he has a functional interest for the reader; he exists to symbolize Fielding's running moral assertion that what appears is all too often accepted as the truth. Or, as Shakespeare might have put it, 'O what a goodly outside falsehood hath!'

Partridge

a fellow of great oddity and humour, which had frequently led him into small inconveniences, such as slaps in the face, kicks in the breech, broken bones, & c

The schoolmaster-cum-barber plays an important role in *Tom Jones*. He is, so to speak, in at the beginning of the plot, denying that he is the father of Tom by Jenny Jones, getting himself into all kinds of domestic trouble, and being set upon by his wife, who dies after his disgrace and their poverty (although that poverty is somewhat eased by Mr Allworthy). As a married man he was born to be henpecked; as an itinerant barber he is given to gossip, some of which, about Sophia, offends Tom. He is credulous, ghosts being part of his life, and he is a man given to physical fear, though he always fights back, whether against his own wife in the early days or against a chambermaid at an inn as he travels with Tom. His speciality is the Latin tag or quote to fit the circumstances, though this is sometimes inaccurate. Partridge's reappearance on the scene gives Fielding the opportunity to indulge his admiration for Cervantes by having Partridge play the Sancho Panza role to an uncomic though wild Don Quixote in the form of Tom Jones.

As the quotation at the heading of this section suggests, Partridge is a great one for getting into scrapes. He is humorous, witty, adept at repartee even when he doesn't understand it. He is greedy for information from Tom, and uses it to good effect and with considerable embroidery when he is in company. Because of his attachment to Tom he is able to give himself airs about his position and about Tom's status. His mouth will always get him into trouble. One of the surprising things is that because of his practical knowledge acquired through experience, he is able to do more for Tom's injuries than the opinionated surgeon who had treated him. From then on Partridge's loyalty to Tom and Tom's appreciation of him and his tolerance of his whims ensures that they will remain together.

Partridge is something of a grotesque, for he is nearly six feet tall. He has a superstitious nature, disliking their night journeys and fearing ghosts at every turn. He is always looking for omens that can be interpreted as affecting their individual fortunes. For most of the time he is able to conceal the fact that he is a Jacobite, so a fine irony plays over his conception. He is given to fear, and the episode with the Old Man of the Hill gives him an opportunity to cut across the main narrative by telling his own ghost story.

Partridge is an opportunist, and is easily taken aside by the young female gypsy; this shows in fact that he is easily duped. But he lives in a kind of insecurity, fears that he has offended Tom, and is terrified during the near robbery on the way to London. When they get there Partridge is employed to find out as much as he can about Sophia; he is adept at finding information, the more sensational the better, as we see from his acquainting Tom with the news, erroneous as it turns out, that Mrs Waters is his mother. His greatest moment is the evening at the play, where his complete involvement in the action, his identifying with character, his fear of ghosts yet again and his running commentary provide genuine humour at the expense of his simple but his essentially likeable rambling. Though reprimanded by Tom for mentioning the robbery, Partridge uncovers the whereabouts of Sophia through Black George, is greatly moved by Tom's imprisonment, and tells his own story to Allworthy in the name of his innocence after all these years.

Square and Thwackum

Square held that human nature was the perfection of all virtue, and that vice was a deviation from our nature in the same manner as deformity of body is. Thwackum, on the contrary, maintained that the human mind, since the Fall, was nothing but a sink of iniquity, till purified and redeemed by grace.

In these characters, whose respective standpoints are given above, Fielding is satirizing extremes of religious practice on the one hand and philosophical theory on the other, in the case of Square of a deistical nature. They are caricatures but with a functional place in the plot, for they contradict each other at every turn, their ideas preconceived rather than rational, and through the exchanges Fielding parodies bloody-mindedness, pedantry and inflexibly fixed ideas.

The result is two thoroughly unpleasant characters whose ambitions dominate their every action, though Square becomes humanized in the course of the plot and ends up with his own confession, which materially changes the face of things for Tom.

Nothing can change Tom's childhood, however, where he is subjected to continual beatings from **Thwackum**, who is a sadist. This is seen early in the narrative when Tom lies about Black George, Blifil gives the game away and is praised by Thwackum, 'whose meditations were full of birch'. At the slightest excuse Tom is flogged, and there is every reason to suppose that he will nurture revenge, which he almost exacts on the occasion when he is discovered with Molly Seagrim in the bushes.

Here we must be fair to Thwackum and say that he shows himself possessed of physical courage. He is sycophantic towards Mr Allworthy, casts his eyes opportunistically on the widow Blifil, always encourages the nauseous creepings of Blifil, and of course covets Mr Allworthy's money. After some time Allworthy sees into and through his 'infirmities', though Fielding is careful to point out that Thwackum does not appear to Allworthy as he does to the reader. Fielding always maintains a sense of perspective in the presentation of character, and will not have Allworthy blamed for employing these two men. There is no doubt that he, and Allworthy, prefer Square, whose failings are human ones, as we shall see.

Thwackum is irascible, easily moved to temper except when he controls it in order to ingratiate himself with Allworthy. Thwackum's most despicable reaction is reserved for the generous legacy of £1000 which Allworthy bequeaths to him when he thinks that he is dying.

Thwackum is unable 'to shut my eyes to my own merit'. He encourages Blifil to tell Allworthy of his mother's death, thus hoping doubtless to bring about Allworthy's own. He is a canting hypocrite, a man who does evil in the name of Christianity. He lacks any humility, is moved only by self interest and believes that scourging, which he enjoys, is the only way to impart Christianity. Fielding does not spare the verbal rod in dealing with him.

Square is humanized by his sins and by his suffering. He is not violent but he is, to use Fielding's word, artful. Like Thwackum, he is an opportunist; unlike Thwackum, he has a conscience. His reasoning early on is always spurious and motivated by self-interest. But although he spots Molly and realizes that he can have her, when he is caught by Tom but not denounced – Tom, like the reader, sees the humour of the situation – he appreciates what has been done. He is careful to keep out of the main situation involving Tom when the latter celebrates Allworthy's recovery, though he is as piqued as Thwackum at the inadequate remuneration which he thinks he will receive as a legacy. Be that as it may, he becomes ill, and his letter to Allworthy is expressive of genuine repentance. There is a kind of nobility in the utterance:

When I reflect on the actions of my past life, I know of nothing which sits heavier on my conscience than the injustice I have been guilty of to that poor wretch, your adopted son. I have not indeed only connived at the villany of others, but been myself active in injustice towards him. (p.824)

This compares very favourably with the attitude of Thwackum, with its concentration on pluralities and the unChristian arrogance of its tone. The philosopher has a conscience; the Christian does not. It would be unwise to read too much into this. What remains remarkable is the power exercised by these two men in the education of the young. I say 'power' since they are able to bring influence to bear which leads to the injustice Square so rightly acknowledges.

Sophia Western

Her mind was every way equal to her person; nay, the latter borrowed some charms from the former: for when she smiled, the sweetness of her temper diffused that glory over her countenance, which no regularity of features can give.

Fielding devotes the second chapter of Book 4 to a full-scale description of Sophia, ransacking the literary analogies so as to present the idealized heroine of his novel. This should be studied in some detail. Sophia fortunately never quite lives up to the description, and this humanizes her, particularly when she is in adversity. She has a tender heart, always susceptible, as she proves over the escape of the small bird; and Tom's attempted rescue, with Blifil's calculated action, conditions her responses to each of them for life.

We are told that she has 'a sprightliness of temper', though there are few occasions when we observe it, for Sophia is demure almost to the point of dullness. She has some markedly redeeming features, though, for she is always polite to servants, almost treating them as equals. This does not show social and moral education as much as genuine sweetness of nature. Naturally she is not consistent in this, and she responds to Honour's alternate commendation of Tom or criticism of him with the moods that reveal her own interest in that fascinating young man. The way she discovers her love is delicately described. When Tom comes to talk to her about something important she has a moment when she feels that he is going to approach her. It turns out that he is asking her to soften her father's attitude towards Black George and his family. But she accepts it with good grace, and exercises her cunning by choosing his favourite music in order to bring her father round to the right frame of mind. Sophia is innocently in love, and her innocence contrasts with the devious, deceptive and immoral attitudes of so many of the characters in *Tom Jones*.

When Tom kisses her hand she is confused, charmed – and, of course, in love. She has to endure his early wildness and insensitivity in pursuing a girl like Molly Seagrim, and offers employment to the girl herself; she charms Tom, though the author observes that she probably doesn't know that she is consciously bent on attracting him. Her father makes things worse for her by suggesting that women will like Tom all the more 'for getting a bastard'. The result is a headache for her and no music for him, and a reprimand for Honour the next day for praising Tom to her as 'so pretty a gentleman'. But Tom saves her at the expense of a broken arm, and there is no escaping the knowledge of her love. Honour's retailing – or distorting – or fabricating – the incident of the muff leads to Sophia's encouraging her servant to talk fully about Tom. In other words, Sophia has all the insecurity of her love. She also fears her father's coming to know of it, but when he flings the muff in the fire (knowing nothing of its importance to her) she hurries to retrieve it.

Sophia, like those two Richardsonian heroines Pamela and Clarissa, is subjected to rough usage and virtual imprisonment once she resists the will of her father and her aunt. Before that, in a manner of speaking, she indicates her preference, for in the bloody battle involving Tom, Thwackum, Blifil and her father she gives Tom 'a look full of inexpressible tenderness' though he has just been caught 'rutting' with Molly Seagrim. But the reaction is too much for her, and she feels faint. With her aunt's misreading of the direction of her affections, Sophia is now tormented; her 'tender sorrow' does not move her aunt, in whose power she is; she begs her father not to force her, but to no avail. A snatched meeting with Tom only confirms the strength of her love, and she shows herself to be a girl of spirit both by the way she treats Blifil and also by her determination to run away. Bribery effectively carries Honour with her.

In her letter to Tom she vows loyalty to him but fears her father's wrath, which she counsels Tom to avoid. She is prostrated when she receives a letter from Tom saying that he must leave her. Honour represents that he has been turned away and, typically and generously, Sophia sends Tom money. She tries to deal with her aunt and her father, and reconciles them at one stage when they have fallen out. The result is that they 'jointly declared war against her'. When she determines to run away and has decided on tactics with Honour, Fielding treats her with some irony; she loves her father so much that in running away she considers she is behaving heroically. On the journey in fact she behaves with great consideration, as she shows when she arrives at the inn. Unfortunately, she hears Partridge's gossip about her dying for the love of Tom. She also discovers that Tom is in bed with Mrs Waters, and in a fit of pique she leaves the muff at the inn for Tom to find. All this after she has said that she is very 'easy'. Sophia is in fact a girl of spirit.

Having met Mrs Fitzpatrick Sophia now goes to another inn where she is suspected of being Jenny Cameron. This throws her into 'a dreadful consternation' and she and Mrs Fitzpatrick go to London where Sophia puts herself under the protection of Lady Bellaston. She is sharp enough in any case to be suspicious of Mrs Fitzpatrick and her designs on the Irish peer. Fielding ironically observes that with Lady Bellaston Sophia is 'into safe hands'. Nothing could be farther from the truth. Lady Bellaston is a scheming and predatory woman who at first responds to Sophia but then abandons her and intrigues to get Tom for herself.

There is one moving sequence at the beginning of Book 13 where Fielding directly connects Sophia with his dead wife Charlotte, but soon the action is joined again. Tom visiting Lady Bellaston finds Sophia returned early from the theatre; despite her surprise, Sophia behaves with spirit, reprimanding him roundly for allowing her name to be bandied about in an inn. Yet it is obvious that she is still in love with him, though she is somewhat disconcerted by the sudden appearance of Lady Bellaston. On being cross-questioned by the latter immediately afterwards, Sophia almost gives away her feelings.

She is refreshingly lacking in the sophistication and hypocrisy of the town at this level of society.

Sophia has the good sense to write to Tom conselling patience. Lady Bellaston's schemes now begin against her. First there is the rumour that Tom is dead, which causes Sophia to faint. The next scheme is to have the weakened Sophia exposed to Lord Fellemar, who will force her to marry him. Sophia in all her innocence reads, and is moved by her reading. But Fellemar's attempt (and it is not that wholehearted, since we know he has scruples) is dramatically interrupted by the arrival of Western. She is now dragged off, and thereafter torn at by the Squire and his sister.

In her confinement, however, she receives the letter from Tom; profoundly moved, she has little time for consideration before her aunt is at her. Nevertheless she writes a letter to Tom which has a grain of optimism – 'Fortune may, perhaps, be sometimes kinder to us both than at present'. It is some time in happening, and before things come right, Sophia has to endure the knowledge of Tom's 'proposal' to Lady Bellaston. This goes deeper than all the shocks of her family's coercion of her, and Tom, in the extremes of his own adversity, receives what seems to be his final rejection by Sophia.

Though she is now depressed beyond measure, Sophia shows a surprising degree of spirit. She flatters her aunt and temporarily reduces that lady's pressure upon her. Mrs Miller's personal appeal moves her, Lord Fellemar's reappearance finds her adamant, and Mr Allworthy's visit finds her treated, as we should expect, with consideration, though she responds by saying that she can never marry Tom. But in the face of his protestations, abject suffering and, it must be observed, emotional and persuasive fluency, Sophia yields. She has spent much of the action suffering and crying, but her spirit has always been in evidence too. She has a kind nature, and a strongly sincere one, and she is loyal and unswerving in her love.

Miss Western

she had attained a very competent skill in politics, and could discourse very learnedly on the affairs of Europe. She was moreover excellently well skilled in the doctrine of amour, and knew better than anybody who and who were together.

Miss Western is presented by Fielding with the delightful irony seen in the quotation above. She has lived at the court, is widely and learnedly read, delights in intrigue, employs the political and war imagery of the time, and uses and abuses her power with abandon. She has no knowledge of the 'simple workings of honest nature' mainly because of her own affectations. Although she is nearly six feet tall she has mastered all the arts of flirtation, and her important function in the plot is to demonstrate that she knows or rather does not know the workings of Sophia's mind. Before we deal with that, let us also say that there is a balance of power between herself and the Squire. Both are aware of the other's fortune, to such an extent that when the Squire has had a difference of opinion with her – this is fairly regular in view of his irascibility and her 'superiority' – he always makes it up, largely because her money is to be left to him. She has a sense of status which is both mercenary and snobbish. At first she supports Blifil's case with Sophia, but she switches with ease to Fellemar, much to the anger of Western, who has no use for the court or, more particularly, what he considers to be the Hanoverian connection.

It is upon Miss Western's misjudgement of Sophia's affections that the whole plot of the novel hinges. She first puts the idea into Western's mind, and then has it put out of her own – to her rage and mortification – by Sophia. The misjudgement is of course the index to her character: wrong-minded, obstinate, short-sighted, scheming, political and intent on furthering her own match-making ambitions and receiving due reward in terms of power for so doing. She is a woman 'of great art' (Fielding means artifice) and thinks erroneously that Sophia is the same. Her sense of family is conveyed when she speaks of Sophia's degrading it by the thought of an alliance with Jones. She immediately acquaints Western with this news. After he has practically imprisoned Sophia at home, Miss Western exerts all her influence to have Sophia delivered into her keeping. She conde-scends to Sophia in terms of her own knowledge of the world. She is like her brother, in that she is not moved by Sophia's tears; failing to influence Sophia, she unleashes her temper on her brother's ignor-ance. She falls completely into the trap of getting Honour dismissed, thus promoting the escape of her niece. It is a further example of her blindness.

When she arrives in London after Western has traced Sophia and again confined her Miss Western, (or 'Mrs' Western as she is called in the fashion of the time), is furious at what she considers his head-strong behaviour. After another row she persuades him to leave everything to her in dealing with Sophia. When Western and Blifil break in upon them she reproves her brother for his lack of decorum. She has other designs now for Sophia in the person of Lord Fellemar, but Sophia's flattery shows that Miss Western is quite a fool when her own past conquests are referred to. As she says, and doubtless delights in saying, 'I was called the cruel Parthenissa.' But Fellemar does come at her invitation, and Sophia is once more subjected to her aunt's vituperation when she refuses to give way. It is typical of Miss Western, however, that she is reconciled to Sophia after the marriage. We get the impression that, despite her acidity at times, she is really anxious for the kind of peace that is really a platform for argument but not for long-term disagreement.

Lady Bellaston

The Queen of the Fairies sends you this;
Use her favours not amiss.

Lady Bellaston is predatory. Having spotted Tom she determines to have him, and uses unscrupulous methods to get him into her power. Tom is rarely able to resist a sexual invitation, even when he is intent upon Sophia. Lady Bellaston uses the latter's name to draw Tom to her at the masquerade, and takes full advantage of the fact that he is poverty stricken to make him her kept man. She is immoral, and undoubtedly indulges her sexual appetites – and the romantic expression of them (judging from her letters) at will. She makes him a present of money, then keeps him dancing attendance upon her while she takes pains to keep Sophia out of his sight. She now pesters him with letters, many of which show her to be in the grip of an infatuation. It seems that she will only be rid of the latter by a proposal of marriage which, with its prospect of tying her down, certainly does not appeal to her.

Her scheme fails when Tom and Sophia are brought into contact with each other as Sophia returns unexpectedly early from the theatre. Lady Bellaston is jealous, and cunningly finds out the state of Sophia's own feelings. She begins to inundate Tom with notes, and gets into a rage when she overhears a conversation between Tom and Honour involving Sophia. She contrives Lord Fellemar's courtship of Sophia, then suggests that he rape her. She sees to it that a rumour is spread that Tom has killed a man in a duel, tries to laugh off the rumour as a joke, and remorselessly carries through her design of the rape by seeing that Sophia is left alone on the following evening.

She is humiliated when Tom fails to respond to an overture of physical love from her because Honour is hidden in the room. But she pretty soon turns this to advantage by employing Honour herself. Lady Bellaston's unscrupulousness, her bluff of sincere love, is called when she is forced to reject Tom's proposal, which had been undertaken at Nightingale's instigation.

Her hatred of Sophia makes her secure Honour to her own service. She now schemes to ruin Tom. She encourages Lord Fellemar's suit, this time with Western, but determines that the best way to remove Tom is to have him press-ganged. She also goes to Miss Western and gets her to support Fellemar's courtship of Sophia, knowing that that lady, unlike her brother, is a snob when it comes to the aristocracy. She damns Jones in the eyes of Miss Western by saying that he has had the impertinence to make love to her (Lady Bellaston). Of course her main stroke here is the letter which Tom has written to her and which, put into Miss Western's hands, is calculated to undermine Sophia when she sees it. The character of Lady Bellaston leaves a nasty taste in the mouth; she is unscrupulous, licentious and despicable.

Other female characters

These form interesting contrasts and cover a wide social range. *Mrs Miller* responds to Tom's goodness and concern with loyalty when he is imprisoned. But there is some individuality in her, since she has the spirit to reprimand him when Lady Bellaston stays late in his room. Her major concern is her daughter, then her poor relations, and she shows how vulnerable she is and how compassionate in each case. Nightingale's desertion of Nancy shows her abject grief; Tom's redressing of this situation provides her with hope and confidence in him. She confides in him, revealing the story of Allworthy's good in the past. *Mrs Fitzpatrick* has something of Lady Bellaston about her. Admittedly, her sufferings at the hands of Mr Fitzpatrick, particularly her imprisonment and the attempts to reduce her, may have embittered her. And at least, like Sophia, she has the courage to flee. But we feel that she lacks the inherent goodness of Sophia, that she is an opportunist who will turn to account anything that comes her way, whether it be an Irish nobleman or the possibility of getting into the good favours of Squire Western. There is a moment too when she definitely fancies Tom, but she lacks the means and, one suspects, the personality, to attract him to her.

Mrs Walters is rather different. The Jenny Jones who was in the confidence of Mrs Blifil and kept her word with regard to the real identity of Tom until she reveals everything to Squire Allworthy, develops into a woman who leads a respectable life with Mr Walters but trusts the villain Northerton and is betrayed for her money. Tom's rescue of her shows that in early middle age she is vulnerable (though most women are to Tom) and that she is sexually attractive. Her affair with Tom is of passing consequence although, naturally enough, it greatly upsets Sophia. Mrs Walters is involved in incidents which reflect her spirit, and she tells the true story that brings Allworthy close to Tom.

Mrs Honour is a superb piece of characterization. She is a calculating opportunist. One is inclined to say that she and Lady Bellaston deserve each other, and I'm not sure that they don't.

Style and modes of narrative in *Tom Jones*

Fielding's style is distinctive, recognizably his and like that of no other writer. His basic narrative method in each of the eighteen books of the novel is to write an introductory chapter, which deals with some facet of art or morality or even involves a glance at the contemporary scene, or at the critics, or a discussion of his own innovatory practice in *Tom Jones*. Fielding is never dull; he writes with verve and gusto, obviously delighting in the creation of his characters and their situations. He moves easily and naturally from the leisured and gentlemanly classical reference or analogy to the earthy and coarse innuendo which characterizes Molly Seagrim's churchyard battle. He can describe an innocence and beauty like Sophia's and embroider it and her with the necessary quotations and literary associations that make her a heroine. At the same time, he pulls no verbal punches when he is launched upon an account of her father and the unrelieved vulgarity and moral limitations of his nature.

This *range* is one of Fieldings's great assets, for variety of interest and a span of difference sustains narrative expectation. Fielding never lets the reader down.

Mock-epic

Tom Jones is a conscious derivation, in parts an imitation, of classical epic as epitomized in Homer's *Iliad* and Virgil's *Aeneid*. But the deliberate presentation is a parody. Epics consist of the accounts of gods or great men, whereas here the hero is a foundling who is brought up by his unknown uncle, expelled from the latter's house, endures a number of scrapes both physical and sexual, and eventually wins through to love and marriage. His battles are not epic; they are frequently sordid, so Fielding has employed the framework of the long poem with its great deeds in a prose structure that deals with the small deeds, obviously with a moral emphasis, of an ordinary man. Fielding however, always has his tongue in his cheek, so that Tom in fact takes on many of the qualities of the hero of epic by virtue of his great physical attractions, his courage, and a certain nobility of conduct that is not undermined by his wildness or by his casual affairs.

Fielding is a comic novelist, but there is an underlying seriousness of intent, which is part of his art, just as in the epics the seriousness is evident from the content and the treatment. Consider the tone of

'With such a smile then, and with a voice, sweet as the evening breeze of Boreas in the pleasant month of November, Mrs Bridget gently reproved the curiosity of Mrs Deborah . . .' (Book 1, Chapter 8, p.71). The area is that of gossip, and the ironic inflation of language underlines the hypocrisy.

Author's Voice

Fielding is the great omniscient presence in his own novels. In the eighteenth and nineteenth centuries it was an accepted part of narrative that the author directed, persuaded, confided, invoked or used rhetorical devices in his interaction with his readers. Fielding is almost the greatest character in his own fiction. He comments on character and situation; he makes comments about contemporaries; he takes us back in time in order to show character development, and often his own voice is employed in a kind of ironic evaluation for the reader.

Of course the opening chapters of each book employ the authorial 'I' in influential directives to the reader. Thus the first chapter in Book 10 finds Fielding telling the reader that 'In the next place we must admonish thee, my worthy friend, (for, perhaps, thy heart may be better than thy head) not to condemn a character as a bad one, because it is not perfectly a good one.' (p.468.) Here the moral tone, and the author's practice, are made equally clear; a true representation of human nature will include both good and bad, and Fielding is here making a modest claim for his realism. He is also attacking those novelists who present characters as either black or white in the moral sense. He makes claims for the permanence of his own writing when he asserts 'As our history doth not, like a newspaper, give great characters to people who were never heard of before, nor will ever be heard of again; the reader may hence conclude, that this excellent woman [Mrs Miller] will hereafter appear to be of some importance in our history.'

It must be admitted that the voice is largely in abeyance towards the end, where the narrative is hurried on at some pace in order to round off the novel – Fielding, despite his humorous chapter headings (see particularly Book 18, Chapter 10 and Chapter The Last) has so many characters to be accounted for.

Classical and Literary

Fielding is one of the most learned of our writers, and classical allusions are strewn throughout the novel. These are not merely confined to the opening chapters of each book, though these often contain full quotations, sometimes accompanied by a translation to make sure that the point is not lost. (See Book 2, Chapter 1, page 87). As R. P. C. Mutter notes, Fielding usually quoted from memory and rarely checked the accuracy of what he wrote. There are references to Aristotle, Socrates, Virgil, Homer, Lucretius, Cicero and Plutarch, to name but a few. The effect is one of a massive background of analogy and reference on which Fielding is drawing in order to give his own work authenticity. But this is admirably complemented by a number of references to Shakespeare, to Pope, to Congreve, to Vanbrugh, to Addison and to Swift. If Fielding has life as his focus, he has literature at his command to provide a commentary on life. And, as with a novelist like Hardy, many of the references are to the less well-known books of his own period, or even to popular romance, which is on the receiving end of his satire.

Satire

The Augustan period in which Fielding wrote was the age of satire. This is perhaps best exemplified in the couplets of Pope, his *Dunciad* representing a sustained attack on the minor poets and 'scribblers' of the period. Fielding's satire takes in contemporary references, seen often in the words he puts into the mouth of Miss ('Mrs') Western, who uses military jargon and constantly refers to the French, thus marking her own court sophistication. Through Western himself, Fielding satirizes the coarse, ignorant, hard-drinking and hard-hunting Tory Squire who has no knowledge of politics but is already disposed to hate anything to do with the King, the Hanoverians, or the Court. Other areas that come in for Fielding's satirical shafts are those of the Law, where the terminology and the pedantry are exposed and, more particularly, the doctor or surgeon. There are two occasions at least where Fielding expatiates at some length on the ignorance and inadequacy of these practitioners, the first being when Tom breaks his arm and is subjected to much greater pain because of the twists and talk of the attendant. The second is when he is badly injured by Northerton, is badly treated by the surgeon and, in addition, is left in a worse state because he has no money.

Society, high society of low moral tone, is exposed in the person of Lady Bellaston, while there are a number of references throughout the text to routs, card-playing, affectations of various kinds and, of course, the central episode of the masquerade. There is too, I feel, satire directed at those who gossip and who judge solely by what appears rather than what is. Thus the landlady and her husband who take Sophia to be Jenny Cameron are being opportunistically Jaco-bites. Fielding himself is strongly anti-Jacobite and one feels that he is castigating this kind of insincerity.

Minor playwrights and poets are satirized somewhat after the manner of Pope and, as I have indicated, Fielding castigates all and every variety of hypocrisy. He satirizes manners, whether those of high society or those of below-stairs society. He makes it very clear that money and inheritance are the roots of evil, and draws a very clear distinction between appearance and reality.

Imagery

Fielding's imagery is wide-ranging. As we have seen, many of the similes and metaphors are deliberately used as parody of the heroic form, but the 18th-century tendency to use nature in rather a stereotyped way is part of Fielding's method. Sometimes he deliber-ately mocks it. He is the master of the telling brief contemporary image that would raise a smile or a grin, as in 'we often suffer him to fortify and entrench himself, like a French army' (Book 5, Chapter 7, p.225). As well as the contemporary imagery there is the classical, which is not used in a mocking way – the employment of the serious analogy to underline a serious point.

Colloquial

Fielding enhances his narrative throughout by a ready recourse to the colloquial, the earthy everyday speech of ordinary people, and again he commands a variety of moods and language. There is the affectedly superior language of, for example, Mrs Honour and Mrs Wilkins, upper servants who have a position to maintain and do so by affectation. Neither can keep it up forever, and the result is lapses into their usual manner of speaking (and pronouncing) or, in the case of Mrs Honour, in the letter she writes to Tom in Chapter 10 of Book 15 (p.732). The colloquial commonplace is seen in the lanaguage of Molly Seagrim and in the landlords and landladies and servants of the various inns that punctuate the progress of Tom and Partridge or Sophia in flight. The soldiers provide another extension of this, but the speech of Mrs Waters probably indicates that her early education with Partridge has not been wasted. Partridge himself speaks a curious mixture of language that reflects his eccentricity, with accu-rate and inaccurate Latin tags thrown in. Fielding can capture nuances of speech and idiosyncrasies, so that the surgeon treating Tom or the one who attends to Sophia are individualized by the pseudo-learned terms that they employ. The range of speech is perhaps best exemplified by another contrast – that between the measured utterance of Squire Allworthy and the impetuous and uncultivated outpourings (which certainly partake of dialect) of Squire Western. Above all, Fielding's language conveys the flavour of the times; it rings true.

Graphic and Descriptive

Fielding can be both landscape descriptive writer (note the account in Book 1, Chapter 4 of the cultivated surroundings of Mr Allworthy's house) and graphic narrator of incident. The latter is his main stylistic device, and we refer again to the immediacy of the fight between Molly Seagrim and those who beset her. Other instances are numerous, and it must be admitted that the fight scenes in *Tom Jones* smack of authorial self-indulgence. He delights in the coarseness and incident they provide, but again one suspects they provide an insight into the nature of uncertain and somewhat lawless times. The attempted robbery gives us certainly some social and moral connection with those times, with the man too impoverished to provide for his family. It says much for Tom's moral priorities that he treats him well both here and later.

There is an element of the salacious in Fielding's graphic narration, as when Tom interrupts the near hanging of Mrs Waters: Fielding focuses – like Tom – on the fact that although she is nearing middle age she has well-formed breasts. The reader is hardly allowed to lose sight of them as she follows Tom but has (pretended) difficulty in covering them up. There is always this tendency in Fielding, and it is seen again when he notes the smirks of the landlord and bystanders when Sophia has a fall. Or the kind of farcical element that involves someone having to be hidden because someone else arrives, as with Mrs Honour and Lady Bellaston. We should not forget that Fielding was an accomplished playwright, and his graphic power testifies to this.

General Questions

1 Select any two or three scenes from the novel in order to illustrate Fielding's graphic descriptive powers.

Guide-line notes for an answer

Introduction The main elements of Fielding's style, very brief, with some mention of playwright capacity for humour, drama, melodrama etc.

Para 1 Tom Jones essentially a novel of scenes, beginning with discovery of Tom, and referring to a few other scenes, which will not be concentrated on here but which have their own effect; for example, Allworthy's interview with Jenny Jones; or Blifil; Tom and Sophia's bird. Then the first major graphic scene – in the churchyard between Molly and those who would put her down.

Para 2 Detail on this scene – coarseness, earthiness (in more ways than one), language, violence, extremes of expression, visual effects, grotesque qualities and any other details the student considers worth including.

Para 3 Another scene – I suggest one of the inn scenes, again with violence, language, vivid interactions etc. Bring out the fact that in Fielding's scenes there is always considerable movement.

Para 4 A scene involving one or two or three individuals only – a good one would be Tom's rescue of Mrs Waters from Northerton, or one of the London scenes such as Tom's rescue of Nightingale from his footman, or the scene involving Tom, Lady Bellaston and Mrs Honour. There is also some graphic description in the scenes in which Sophia is reduced either by her father or, in a different way by her aunt. A good humorous scene would be the visit to see the production of *Hamlet*.

Para 5 Conclusion – the main effects of a Fielding scene – the feeling that you are *there*, the strong sense of immediacy, the visual and verbal effects.

2 Write a character study of Tom, bringing out both the 'wildness' and the sensitivity in his personality.

3 In what ways do you think that Sophia is 'over-idealized'? You should refer closely to the text in your answer.

4 Write an essay on Fielding's use of the mock-heroic in *Tom Jones*. What does it contribute to our appreciation of the novel?

5 Write an essay on the variety of Fielding's humour in *Tom Jones*.

6 Compare and contrast Thwackum and Square.

7 In what ways do you find Squire Western and his sister unsympathetic characters?

8 In what ways is *Tom Jones* a picture of life at the time? Refer to the text in support of your views.

9 'The novel is mainly about money.' How far would you agree or disagree with this statement about *Tom Jones*?

10 Write an essay on the role played by either Mrs Miller or Mrs Waters or Lady Bellaston in *Tom Jones*.

11 In what ways is Partridge an important character in *Tom Jones*?

12 What are the main objects of Fielding's satire and irony in *Tom Jones*?

13 'The introduction of the Man on the Hill spoils the narrative tension of the novel.' Discuss.

14 In what ways is Fielding a moralist? You should refer closely to the text in your answer.

15 Write on any aspect of *Tom Jones* not covered by the essays above but which you consider to be important to our appreciation of the novel.

Further Reading

Henry Fielding, *Joseph Andrews*
Wilbur L. Cross, *The History of Henry Fielding* (Yale)
Ian Watt, *The Rise of the Novel* (Chatto and Windus)
Andrew Wright, *Henry Fielding: Mask and Feast* (Chatto and Windus)
Neil Compton ed., *Tom Jones: a Casebook* (Macmillan)

Brodie's Notes

D. H. Lawrence	**The Rainbow**
D. H. Lawrence	**Sons and Lovers**
D. H. Lawrence	**Women in Love**
Harper Lee	**To Kill a Mockingbird**
Laurie Lee	**Cider with Rosie**
Christopher Marlowe	**Dr Faustus**
Arthur Miller	**The Crucible**
Arthur Miller	**Death of a Salesman**
John Milton	**Paradise Lost**
Robert C. O'Brien	**Z for Zachariah**
Sean O'Casey	**Juno and the Paycock**
George Orwell	**Animal Farm**
George Orwell	**1984**
J. B. Priestley	**An Inspector Calls**
J. D. Salinger	**The Catcher in the Rye**
William Shakespeare	**Antony and Cleopatra**
William Shakespeare	**As You Like It**
William Shakespeare	**Hamlet**
William Shakespeare	**Henry IV Part I**
William Shakespeare	**Julius Caesar**
William Shakespeare	**King Lear**
William Shakespeare	**Macbeth**
William Shakespeare	**Measure for Measure**
William Shakespeare	**The Merchant of Venice**
William Shakespeare	**A Midsummer Night's Dream**
William Shakespeare	**Much Ado about Nothing**
William Shakespeare	**Othello**
William Shakespeare	**Richard II**
William Shakespeare	**Romeo and Juliet**
William Shakespeare	**The Tempest**
William Shakespeare	**Twelfth Night**
George Bernard Shaw	**Pygmalion**
Alan Sillitoe	**Selected Fiction**
John Steinbeck	**Of Mice and Men** and **The Pearl**
Jonathan Swift	**Gulliver's Travels**
Dylan Thomas	**Under Milk Wood**
Alice Walker	**The Color Purple**
W. B. Yeats	**Selected Poetry**

ENGLISH COURSEWORK BOOKS

Terri Apter	**Women and Society**
Kevin Dowling	**Drama and Poetry**
Philip Gooden	**Conflict**
Philip Gooden	**Science Fiction**
Margaret K. Gray	**Modern Drama**
Graham Handley	**Modern Poetry**
Graham Handley	**Prose**
Graham Handley	**Childhood and Adolescence**
R. J. Sims	**The Short Story**